HACKABLE

HACKABLE

HOW TO DO
APPLICATION
SECURITY RIGHT

TED HARRINGTON

LIONCREST
PUBLISHING

HACKABLE
How to Do Application Security Right

ISBN   978-1-5445-1767-4   *Hardcover*
       978-1-5445-1766-7   *Paperback*
       978-1-5445-1765-0   *Ebook*

To Mom and Dad, for inspiring me to serve others.
This book is a result of that ethos.

CONTENTS

To those who seek excellence:
this book is for you.

You are not alone.

WHY SECURE YOUR APP?

LIE
Security is a headache.

TRUTH
Security is a competitive advantage.

You're at the beach. You pick up a grain of sand and then toss it back. Later, your friend goes to the same beach and picks up a grain of sand. What are the chances that it's the same one you picked up?

Pretty unlikely, right?

Now multiply that by every beach on earth. And multiply *that* by a gazillion earths. That's what cryptographers might call "statistical improbability." It gives you a sense of how unlikely it is that anyone—human or machine—could guess the private key that secures a cryptocurrency wallet.[1] Keys simply can't be predicted.

---

1   Technically, the probability is 1 in 115 quattuorvigintillion (2^{256}). So, yeah, it's not gonna happen.

Or can they?

Well, we did. A bunch of times, in fact.

We published security research on Ethereum wallets that discovered a flaw in how the software provisions private keys. The flaw enabled us to successfully predict 732 of them.[2]

That's like picking up your exact grain of sand 732 times! It shouldn't be possible *once*, let alone *hundreds* of times!

A crucial component of what keeps cryptocurrency wallets secure is the statistical improbability that anyone could guess the private key. Weak keys mean that wallets—and all the currency in them—are vulnerable. If exploited, an attacker could access the accounts, transfer funds, and do anything else the legitimate owner of the wallet could do. When there's a weak key protecting a cryptocurrency wallet, it's like a pile of cash is sitting on a sidewalk. Someone is going to steal it eventually.

And someone did.

We discovered that literally every single unit of currency that was once kept in those 732 vulnerable wallets had been transferred out. All of it was funneled into a single destination wallet. We had clearly stumbled upon a hacking campaign in progress.

It gets even crazier. It wasn't a small amount of money that was stolen either. Quite a bit, actually: $54,343,407.

Fifty-four million dollars! The scope of the theft was substantial.

Next, we wanted to see how quickly vulnerable wallets are looted. To answer that, we put $1 of our own Ethereum into

---

2 Read it here: Independent Security Evaluators, "The Blockchain Bandit: Finding over 700 Active Private Keys on Ethereum's Blockchain," April 23, 2019, https://www.ise.io/casestudies/ethercombing/.

one of the vulnerable wallets to see what would happen. Almost instantly, the money was gone. Snap your finger, and that's how quickly our money was transferred to the same wallet where the rest of the stolen money had gone.

This thief—whom we dubbed Blockchain Bandit—was actively stealing from vulnerable wallets. The massive theft was achieved by exploiting the same vulnerability our research had discovered.[3]

This story powerfully demonstrates two simple facts. First, software flaws exist. Second, attackers exploit them.

Stories like this are both unexpected and yet not uncommon. Applications are exploited every single day. It's why this book needs to exist.

Application security is the process of finding, fixing, and preventing security vulnerabilities in order to improve the security of an application.[4] Security vulnerabilities are weaknesses that an attacker can exploit in order to perform unauthorized actions within a computer system.

The question is not whether vulnerabilities exist in your application—they do. Your vulnerabilities exist. No, the real question is simply which happens first: will attackers exploit them, or will you fix them?

It needs to be you.

---

3 You can read the wild, true story in *Wired*'s exposé on our research here: Andy Greenberg, "A 'Blockchain Bandit' Is Guessing Private Keys and Scoring Millions," *Wired*, April 23, 2019, https://www.wired.com/story/blockchain-bandit-ethereum-weak-private-keys/.

4 There are tons of terms in application security. Each term is defined as we go, but if you ever need a refresher, there's a handy glossary at the end of the book.

That's why you're holding this book in your hands. It's your responsibility to make sure that the software your company develops is secure. Until security is done right, you accept unnecessary risk, while security gets in the way of sales.

You need to reduce risk. You need to win sales.

There's just one problem, though...

SECURITY IS A MINEFIELD

Sometimes companies approach security as if it's a necessary evil, something they don't want to do but know they must.[5] When that happens, security fails to be a priority, which turns it into a blind spot. Complicating this, there's a lot of misinformation out there (which is why each chapter in this book opens with a "lie" and then a "truth" you should replace it with).

Many companies don't know which security approaches work and which don't. Other companies don't even know where to start. They aren't sure what to assess, what to prioritize, or how much to spend. They don't know how hackers think or break systems. They don't know the best way to find their vulnerabilities. They don't know the best way to fix them.

Worse, companies sometimes think they *do* know those things, only to later learn they were actually doing it *wrong* the entire time.

Here are some of the most common problems that companies face—or *think* they face—when approaching security:

---

5   This book refers almost exclusively to "companies." However, almost all of the ideas, strategies, and tactics apply the same to nonprofits, government agencies, and other organizations that aren't commercial businesses.

- Their developers juggle many priorities. Security is just one. Yet, usually, the top levels of leadership determine which priorities to emphasize. When leadership doesn't understand or prioritize security, their developers simply can't allocate sufficient time to it.

- Security isn't the primary focus of their training either. Developers are usually brilliant people trying to build clean, efficient, effective code. They're not always thinking about how to break it. By contrast, attackers spend every waking minute studying how to break that clean, efficient, effective code.

- Companies tend to believe that security slows down development. As a result, deadlines cause security to get postponed. This just causes regressions and rework later. It makes things harder and more expensive in the long run.

- Security sometimes complicates the user experience, yet users demand simplicity.

- Security sometimes interrupts the sales process. Security questionnaires (those seemingly annoying attempts by their customers to document security postures, policies, and controls) are time-consuming, confusing, and poorly written. Sometimes they aren't even relevant. Meanwhile, requests for proposals (RFPs) demand thoroughly detailed security responses.

- Security is never done. Companies don't know if "good enough" is actually good enough. They're not sure when they can move on.

- Change is the only constant. As technology shifts, so too does the security model. Software development itself is changing.

- Too many terms mean too many things to too many people. There's a severe lack of uniformity on what security testing is or should be. This confusion makes it even harder to translate outcomes to the chief executive officer (CEO), the board, and your customers.[6]

- Certain types of security testing deliver reports that border on unusable. They're packed with false positives (suggesting there's a vulnerability where there's not one) and inappropriate severity ratings. They report the same, duplicate issues multiple times. There's no context for the unique threat model, they fail to account for risk appetite, and they don't give tailored advice on how to fix the issues.

- Budgets are limited, and available security talent is scarce.

---

6 For the sake of simplicity, "customers" is used throughout the book to refer to either your current customers whom you already work with, your prospective customers whom you're trying to work with, or both.

- They feel like they don't know what they don't know and are uncertain how to resolve that or even where to begin.

To do security right, it requires time, attention, and money. However, you have many other priorities competing for those same resources. Further complicating things is the cold reality that security might not even be your whole job. Regardless, if there's a security breach, it's still on *you*. You don't want to have to explain to anyone why you suffered a security breach. You've read the headlines: Twitter, Zoom, British Airways, Google, T-Mobile, Cathay Pacific, Timehop, Panera Bread, Facebook, Sears, Kmart, Best Buy, Fortnite, and First American Financial have all had their apps hacked. You don't want to be next.

You wish application security was easier. You wish this wasn't your problem.

You just want to be secure.

Sound familiar?

If so, I know how you feel. I've been in the trenches with many people battling these same challenges. I understand why you might think security is a headache, but in reality, security is your best friend. It's not just the *right thing* to do; it also delivers a competitive advantage for your business. Proving that you're secure in the face of unknown threats is *exactly* how you earn the trust of your customers. That leads to more sales, more customers, and more market share. It's how you become a leader in your field.

Sadly, most people don't do security right. But after you read this book, you will.

That, my friend, is a competitive advantage. Your customers want to use software that is secure. When you can deliver that but your competitors can't, *you'll win.*

The ultimate outcome of security done right

This book is about securing software. That means securing both web applications (those built to use via a web browser) and native applications (those built specifically for mobile or desktop use). It includes firmware, embedded systems, and anything related to the Internet of Things (the system of computing devices that's connected to the internet, often referred to simply as IoT). It includes how you design and then secure your cloud deployments. It includes all of the crucial components, from code to executables to application programming interfaces (APIs). Most applications have dependencies, so this domain also includes how you integrate with third-party systems, libraries, and shared components. Whether your solution is hosted on-site or in the cloud, this book is for you. Application security is more than just running scanners. It includes the many different things you'd do to secure your systems, such as security assessments, security consulting, design analysis, reverse engineering, secure software development, and more.

The approach to all of that is actually much easier than you may think. There's a method to the madness, and I'm going to show you exactly what it is. I'll also give you all the information you need to make sure your higher-ups agree to invest the time and money for you to be able to do it right.

At first, you may think you need security testing, which you do, but it's more than that. You may also think you need security consultants, the experts who help solve your application security problems, including not just testing but also design, coding, security principles, and more.[7] That's also true, but again, it's more than that. Getting security right is an attitude. It's a mindset. It's a pursuit of excellence. You want to write the best code. You want to build the best product. That means you need to get security right, too. You can't do it entirely in-house, and you can't entirely outsource it either.

Security can feel uncertain, but it doesn't need to be that way. This book ensures that you *will* get security right. When you do security right, you create order out of this chaotic mess. You turn uncertainty into certainty. You achieve confidence that your approach is working. You discover your catastrophic vulnerabilities. You fix them. You become more effective and more efficient. You use time better. You spend money better.

You build better, more secure products.

You gain a competitive advantage.

You earn trust.

You win sales.

WHAT YOU'LL LEARN

There's a lot of advice out there about how to approach application security. Some of it is even good advice. Much of it, though, is straight-up wrong. (Now, if you're like me, a statement like

---

7   Throughout the book, the following terms are used interchangeably: security consultant, security evaluator, security partner, security assessor, and security expert. These terms all refer to the person or group outside of your company who help you make good security decisions and improve the security of your system.

that makes you question whether the advice in this book is, in fact, correct. Good! I'll get to that in a moment.)

I'll help you rethink norms. Then I'll teach you the best way to find security vulnerabilities. Then I'll share the best approach for fixing them. That's how you get secure. Once you are secure, you need to prove it. I'll help you do that, too.

You'll learn everything you need to know in order to do application security right. Here's just a sample of the how-to topics covered in this book:

- How to think like an attacker

- How to multiply impact with both in-house personnel and external experts

- How to pick a methodology: white-box versus black-box

- How to figure out if you need penetration testing or something else

- How to find your security vulnerabilities, including especially the unknowns and custom exploits

- How to fix your security vulnerabilities

- How to approach reassessments and deal with change

- How to determine how much money to spend

- How to establish a threat model

- How to build security into the development process

- How to use security to drive sales

WHY LISTEN TO ME?

This book isn't about me; it's about you. It's about your problems and how to solve them. However, to make sure you can do that, let me briefly explain why you can trust me.

I know how hackers think, and I know how to defend against them. I know these things because I'm on the front lines of ethical hacking.

My name is Ted Harrington, and along with my business partner Stephen Bono, we own the security consulting firm Independent Security Evaluators (ISE). Our company is made up of ethical hackers, computer scientists, reverse engineers, cryptographers, software developers, penetration testers, and security consultants. We specialize in security assessments (helping find and fix security vulnerabilities) and security consulting (helping solve complex security engineering problems). Since 2005, we've helped hundreds of companies discover (and then fix) tens of thousands of security vulnerabilities. The stories in this book are their stories.

Security research is in our blood. The company was born out of the PhD program at Johns Hopkins University. In our first piece of research, we built a weaponized software radio to hack the onboard computer in a car and then start it without the authentic key. We were the first company to hack the iPhone and the first company to hack Android OS. We broke new ground hacking medical devices, IoT devices, password managers, and cryptocurrency wallets.

Our research has discovered vulnerabilities in products by Apple, Google, Equifax, Verizon, ExxonMobil, PayPal, Ford Motors, General Electric, Toyota Financial, Liberty Mutual, Allstate, ADP, GEICO, PNC Bank, and MetLife.

Our work has appeared in hundreds of news outlets, including *The New York Times*, *The Wall Street Journal*, *The Washington Post*, *USA Today*, *Financial Times*, *Wired*, and *CBS News*.

We started IoT Village, a hands-on hacking event that's facilitated the discovery of more than three hundred previously unknown security vulnerabilities. The winners of our hacking contests have been awarded the elusive DEF CON Black Badge, which is the security community's version of a Hall of Fame jacket. This has happened not once, not twice, but three times (and we're trying to keep getting better so it can happen again).

I'm not telling you this to brag. I'm telling you this so you can trust that the information in this book is accurate and proven. The bottom line is that we know what we're doing, and we've been doing it for a long time. Literally everything in this book has been field-tested by ethical hackers. All of it is backed by research. It's all proven to work for both large enterprises and funded startups (and everyone in between).

It will work for you, too.

I've learned many things from the companies I've been fortunate to serve, three of which stand out. First, security is hard to justify, let alone do. Companies commonly overlook the competitive advantage that a well-secured solution has over a poorly secured one: your customers want the software that they use to be secure. However, most companies fail miserably in securing their solutions, let alone proving it. Our clients have all seen security as the massive business opportunity it is and capitalized on it.

Second, most people see the way things are *supposed to work*, yet attackers see the way things are *not supposed to work*. That's where exploits live. It's imperative that companies fill in this massive blind spot, yet it's immensely difficult to do. Most companies don't even know where to begin, and there simply aren't enough skilled people in the world to do it.

Third, most companies are not going deep enough to find and fix their issues—but often don't realize it. Until we arrived on the scene, many of our clients believed they were doing security right, too. Once we showed them the better way, they were shocked to learn they'd only been going surface-deep, even when they *thought* they were being thorough. That disconnect is disorienting, and I want to help resolve it.

I see these problems every day, so I knew I needed to write this book. If the smart, competent, capable people I get to call my clients struggle with these issues, I know that tons more people are struggling, too. This book is my attempt to expand my impact and make a bigger difference. I've spent years acquiring this knowledge, and it feels irresponsible to do anything other than share it as broadly as possible. For that reason, this book is packed with exactly the same guidance we give our clients. Just like it helps them, I hope it will help you, too.

Here's the bottom line: *security matters*.

There can be a negative lens to this. Security matters because without it, your mission is at risk. It matters because there are very bad people who don't care about you or your mission or the way you're going to make a mark on the world. But they do care about abusing you in order to achieve their own goals. And they are *relentless*. It matters because it's embarrassing, expensive, and business-threatening to suffer a security breach.

More importantly, there can be a positive lens, too. Security matters because it gives you a chance to differentiate from your competition, gain a competitive edge, and grow your business. It matters because human beings love solving hard problems, and security is nothing but hard problems. It feels good when you do it correctly. It matters because when you do it right, you look good, and wonderful career opportunities present themselves to you. It matters because *you* matter: many people rely on you to do your job, keep the technology secure, and ensure that the company marches toward its goals. If you do your job well, you serve them all—including especially the ones who don't realize they're relying on you. Battling faceless enemies and unknown threats in a job where success is often measured as simply "we didn't get hacked yet" can be thankless. So let me be the first to say thank you. It matters because *it's the right thing to do*.

My security friends sometimes refer to ethical hacking as "good guys doing bad guy stuff." I love that framing because of how authentically human—and accurate—it is. More specifically, ethical hacking is the act of probing technology for weaknesses by using the same tools and techniques that malicious actors use in order to assess and improve the security of a system. The key difference is that the *motivation* for ethical hacking is to help, not hurt. It's done *legally* and *ethically*. It's the process of *thinking* like an attacker in order to *defend* against the attacker. In the media, the term "hacker" has come to mean a bad person associated with evildoing. That's not entirely accurate.

"Hacker" simply refers to someone who solves problems and makes things behave differently than intended. Ethical hackers do good; attackers do bad. Both are hackers.

The good hackers and bad hackers all start from the same place: They both dig to find weaknesses. They both determine how to exploit those weaknesses. That's where there's a fork in the road, though: attackers *exploit* the system, whereas ethical hackers *fix* it. Ethical hackers have all the skills to do damage but instead choose to make things better. Ethical hackers are like a coach for professional athletes: you're already excellent at what you do, and it's our job to evaluate your form and guide you through the hard work of improving it. The competition—your collection of attackers—is doing the same thing, but they're not trying to *improve* your form; they're trying to *take advantage* of it. Both teams want to win, but the question is simply, which one will? That's why you need the best coaches on your team.

Ethical hacking comes both as a contracted service (where the company pays for the guidance, but the findings are strictly confidential) or as research (where the ethical hackers aren't paid but can publish the findings). In either case, the goal is the same: *make things better*. The stories in this book come from both forms of ethical hacking. The stories deliver the exact insights you need to do security right.

It's all proven to work.

It will work for you, too.

WHAT THIS BOOK IS AND IS NOT

This book is a prescriptive, pragmatic guide. It tells you what to do, how to do it, and why. It identifies—and then shatters—

misconceptions, falsehoods, and mistaken beliefs that hold many security programs back.

It's written for technology leaders, such as the chief technology officer (CTO), chief information officer (CIO), chief information security officer (CISO), vice president of engineering, head of development, engineering director, security architect, product manager, lead developer, and many other technologists and security professionals. It's also for those of you rising into these roles someday. If your role is to build better, more secure systems, this book is for you. It's for seasoned execs, newbies, and everyone in between.

There are harsh truths in here. I shine a spotlight on how people, including maybe even you, are doing it wrong. I do this not to shame anyone but to help you get better so you can do application security right.

This book is not for everyone. It's not for anyone seeking a code-level technical deep dive. It's about application security, not other security domains (although application security is the soft underbelly to almost all of them).

You'll find that I speak in plain, simple terms, using lots of stories and metaphors. I do this because application security is already complex enough—you don't need me making it any harder to understand. You need me to make it *easier*. Some readers may find the language to be too simple, while others might still be confused by the terms. Hopefully, you find the narrative to be accessible, but if you ever get tripped up by a term (of which there is *a lot*), you can find it defined in the glossary.

The fact that you're reading a book like this means that you're a smart, capable person, striving to get better. Unfortunately, you've probably dealt with security professionals at some point who didn't treat you that way. You've probably heard one of them suggest that your "baby" (the innovative technology you're building) is ugly.

But it's not about where you are *now*; it's about where you are *going*. Yes, you'll find that you made mistakes—and that's exactly the point! That's a *good* thing, not a *bad* thing. The entire point of this book is to help you deal with those mistakes. It's about getting better. It's about finding your vulnerabilities before the bad guy does. It's about fixing them before your attacker exploits them.

You won't find a cure-all in this book. There's no panacea, no silver bullet, no "easy" button, no "get secure quick" scheme because no such thing exists. Security is an investment, and like any investment, this one requires effort, time, and money. You won't learn how to become "unhackable," because that is neither possible nor even the right goal.

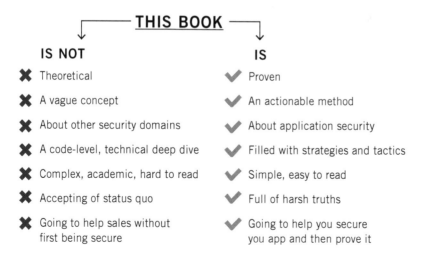

THIS BOOK

IS NOT	IS
✖ Theoretical	✔ Proven
✖ A vague concept	✔ An actionable method
✖ About other security domains	✔ About application security
✖ A code-level, technical deep dive	✔ Filled with strategies and tactics
✖ Complex, academic, hard to read	✔ Simple, easy to read
✖ Accepting of status quo	✔ Full of harsh truths
✖ Going to help sales without first being secure	✔ Going to help you secure you app and then prove it

This book extracts insights from the front lines of ethical hacking. It simplifies those insights and translates them into an actionable method. It does this so that you can be better.

If this resonates, then this is the right book for you.

Let's get started.

CHAPTER 1

START WITH THE RIGHT MINDSET AND THE RIGHT PARTNER

LIE
We're good.

TRUTH
We could be better.

N o, security is not like insurance.

This is a common comparison people make, suggesting that security is like insurance because, as one technology executive said, "It's a necessary evil. You gotta do it, even if you don't want to."[8]

However, it's a poor analogy. Insurance delivers no benefit

---

8 Throughout the book, you'll see real quotes by real technology executives, developers, and security professionals. These came either from interviews for this book or in the course of my life as a security consultant.

until something bad happens; security delivers tremendous benefits throughout the process. Insurance doesn't prevent bad things; security does.

This comparison has always bothered me because it's usually framed to marginalize the positive and powerful impact security has on your mission. My life's work is defined by four principles: do hard things, do things that matter, do things in the service of others, and get better every day. All four are central to the pursuit of security (and these principles drove me to write this book for you). I can't reconcile how those factors could exist in security if it's nothing more than a "necessary evil."

Don't get me wrong: insurance is a great thing. It protects you from financial ruin when something bad happens. But security really isn't like insurance at all. Instead, security is like *fitness*. When you do it right, you get better, stronger, and less susceptible to issues that plague everyone else. You look good. You feel good. Others are attracted to you. You join a community of enthusiasts.

But it's not easy. There are no shortcuts. What you put in is what you get out. It doesn't end; it's an ongoing process. Becoming fit starts with your mindset and how well you leverage experts to achieve explosive results. It's the same with security.

Security starts with the right mindset,
combined with the right partnership.

This chapter ensures that you'll be able to successfully execute the methods, strategies, and tactics you'll learn throughout the book. There are two parts to this. First, we'll explore the successful security mindset: constantly seek improvement and think like a hacker. Then we'll explore how to apply that mindset in ways that multiply impact: by leveraging both in-house and external security experts. Taken together, the right mindset and the right partnership enable you to achieve everything in this book.

MINDSET PART 1:
CONSTANTLY SEEK IMPROVEMENT

You need to prove that your app is secure. Whether you need to prove it to your customers, to your boss, or even just to yourself, you accomplish this by finding security vulnerabilities and then fixing them.

To do that, you may think you just need security testing, such as "penetration testing" or "red teaming."[9] However, while you do indeed need security testing, you won't get it right unless your goal is to achieve security excellence. Security excellence is the relentless pursuit of *better*. It's about constant improvement. Wherever you are today, be better tomorrow. And then be better the day after that, and the month after that, and the year after that. Don't wait. Start getting better *right now*.

That's the heart of security excellence, and security excellence is the heart of application security. It's the mindset that leads to security success. You must understand it. You must apply it.

Think of all the ways that Apple has changed the world, whether with computers, music, or phones. They're certainly defined by *overall* excellence. They're also defined by *security* excellence.

---

9 Most people use these terms wrong. We'll get to that.

When Apple first launched the iPhone, our research team wanted one badly—partly because it's awesome, but also because we wanted to hack it. And we wanted to be first.

Problem was, so did every other security researcher. We didn't have any advantage over anyone. It was a level playing field. We couldn't get our hands on the device before the release to the general public. Apple wouldn't reveal anything in advance about what the new system might entail. We couldn't even skip the line to buy one! We had to camp out in front of the store, just like every other fanatic.

Without early access to the device, it would simply be a race. That was too much of a toss-up. What we needed to do was to create an advantage. We needed to tip the scales in our favor and give ourselves a head start. To do that, we leaned on a simple theory: in the rush to launch by release date, Apple might accidentally port an unresolved security flaw from the desktop operating system to the mobile operating system. We guessed that other researchers wouldn't consider this angle, and so if we were right, it would give us the advantage we needed. We could consider exploit scenarios in advance, enabling us to be a few steps ahead once we got a device.

Our hunch proved correct.

Apple did indeed carry an unresolved issue over to the mobile operating system: a buffer overflow vulnerability. It's a flaw whereby attackers can corrupt memory in order to manipulate system functionality—and it delivered full administrative control of the device.[10] We could modify contacts, send text mes-

---

10 To read the technical details, you can download the original research here: Independent Security Evaluators, "Exploiting the iPhone,"...

sages, delete photos—anything a user can do, we could do. It represented a catastrophic compromise. Unquestionably, it was a worst-case scenario for Apple.

To prove the concept, we took over the iPhone of a *New York Times* reporter while it sat on his desk in Manhattan, two hundred miles away from our lab in Baltimore (don't worry, this was done in collaboration with him as part of the research). As you might imagine, it was quite a vivid demonstration. It made for a great news story.

We achieved our goal, becoming the first company ever to hack the iPhone. But that's not where the story ends; after all, the entire point of security research is to make things better. We reported the issue to Apple and helped them figure out how to fix it. They issued a patch, eradicating the vulnerability. Millions of people buying iPhones were now safe from this particular flaw.

The key is *getting better*. Apple, even with all of its money and ridiculously smart people, still introduces vulnerabilities. They're human just like the rest of us. Yet, this story displayed a few qualities you want to emulate: they fixed their product and made it better. They set out not just to build good products but to build *secure* products. And they recognized that this work is never done.

That's how you need to think and behave, too.

...July 12, 2017, https://www.ise.io/casestudies/exploiting-the-iphone/. Read the original story from *The New York Times* here: John Schwartz, "IPhone Flaw Lets Hackers Take Over, Security Firm Says," *The New York Times*, July 23, 2007, https://www.nytimes.com/2007/07/23/technology/23iphone.html.

MINDSET PART 2: THINK LIKE A HACKER

To defend against attackers, you need to think like them. Here's the basic premise:

- Normal users figure out what they're *supposed* to do.

- Attackers figure out what they're *not supposed* to do. Then they do those things.

Attackers relentlessly look for flaws. They identify assumptions, break systems, and ask "what-if" questions.

Let me explain with a metaphor. A while back, I went to a bar. There was a long line and a twenty-dollar cover charge to get in. Yuck! I wanted to avoid both of those. Instead of waiting in line like everyone else, I walked up to the VIP hostess and confidently declared:

"Hello! I'm on the VIP list." The truth, however, is that I was not on the list.

She replied, "Hi! What's your name?"

"I'm with the party," I said vaguely. I was not actually with any party, but I wanted her to believe that I was.

"Which one?"

"The big one," I said, once again being vague. I gambled that one group was bigger than the others.

"Oh," she said, flipping through her list, "the Smith party?"

Bingo.

"Yes." I smiled. "I'm with the Smith party."

"Great, right this way."

With that, she opened the velvet rope, escorted me past the cashier, and welcomed me to the bar.

Access granted! I broke the system. I was a regular visitor who was given elevated privileges. I certainly didn't achieve that by thinking like a normal person. Not at all. I did it by thinking like an attacker.

This metaphor is a classic example of social engineering (tricking people into taking actions they otherwise shouldn't) rather than a technical exploit. However, it nevertheless vividly demonstrates the attacker mindset. You must apply the same ideas to break your application. Simply replace "bar" with "application," and this story shows exactly how to think like an attacker. They don't *follow* the rules; they figure out how to *break* them.

Here's how:

1. **Set a goal.** In this story, the goal was to bypass the line and the cover charge. To do that, I needed to elevate my privileges from a normal patron to VIP.

2. **Learn how the system works.** For example, I observed that the bar required authorization, which is when a system verifies permission to do something (in this case, enter by the VIP line). The purpose of the VIP host is to verify those permissions.

3. **Gather information.** To get on the VIP list, I needed to identify a group who was legitimately on it so I could associate myself with that group.

4. **Identify assumptions.** The system relied on several assumptions. Some groups have VIP access. A person is authorized to enter by the VIP line if they are with a valid VIP group. A person is assumed to be part of a VIP group if they can produce the group's name.

5. **Get the system to respond in ways it's not supposed to.** By using specially crafted inputs (my vague, leading statements, paired with my confident demeanor), I got the VIP hostess to reveal secrets, such as the name of a valid VIP group. I then got her to believe that I was a member of that group. She was supposed to keep me out, but as a result of this, she let me in instead.

6. **Exploit.** I escalated my privileges from normal patron to VIP, thereby obtaining elevated access I shouldn't have had. I entered the bar without paying cover or waiting in line. The system was specifically designed to prevent exactly this, and yet I was able to do it anyway—all by thinking like an attacker.

Now let's apply the idea to a technical exploit. Back when he was in the PhD program at Johns Hopkins University, my business partner Steve and a few of his colleagues learned about an anti-theft mechanism known as the car immobilizer. It's a radio frequency identification (RFID) system that many major car brands such as Nissan, Mazda, and Ford use in their ignition sequence. It verifies that you have the authentic key before the onboard computer allows the engine to start.

It was widely considered to be *unhackable*.

Needless to say, Steve and his fellow security researchers declared, "Challenge accepted!"

To disprove this preposterous claim and prove that this system was indeed *hackable* and that, by extension, any system is *hackable*, they needed to understand how the system was *supposed* to work and make it behave differently. They wanted to see if they could start a car without the authentic key.

To do that, they needed to defeat the communications between the ignition key and the onboard computer. The security of that system relied on two things:

(a) the secrecy of the cryptographic algorithm, which is the mathematical process for encrypting and decrypting data; and

(b) the secrecy of the encryption key, which is a small secret piece of information that the cryptographic algorithm uses to protect the larger stream of data.

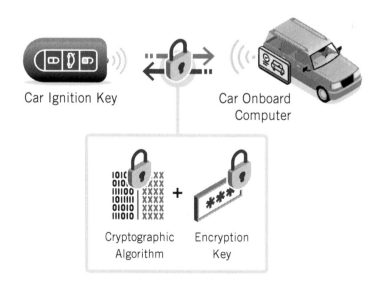

Car Ignition Key   Car Onboard Computer

Cryptographic Algorithm   +   Encryption Key

First, the research team focused on the cryptographic algorithm. They set out to reverse engineer it, a process to deconstruct a component in order to learn how it works, and figure out how to defeat it. It turns out that rather than using a standard protocol for the cryptographic algorithm, the manufacturer had built their own. I beg you: *please don't do that!* Standard protocols are heavily hardened thanks to the extensive effort invested by countless organizations over long periods of time.

But when you build your own, you're on your own.

When you build your own cryptographic protocol, you're starting over from scratch in terms of eradicating weaknesses in it. As a result, unknown weaknesses will exist. You need to replicate the years of testing delivered by a broad range of experts in order to harden your new protocol. However, you probably don't have the time, money, or breadth of expertise for that. This means that custom cryptographic protocols tend to be much, much easier to crack than standard protocols. Because this system used a custom protocol that did indeed have some weaknesses, the research team was able to easily reverse engineer it.

Next, the research team worked to break the encryption key. It turns out that it was comically small: a mere forty bits. It was trivial to defeat with a brute-force attack, a systematic process of attempting every possible decryption pair. All they needed was a few hundred dollars' worth of off-the-shelf computing components and a few weeks to run the attack.

With both the cryptographic algorithm and the encryption key defeated, they built a weaponized software radio to communicate with the vehicle. Then they inserted a mechanical copy of the ignition key and turned it. The immobilizer was supposed to prevent ignition without the authentic key, but the car started anyway.

And just like that, they hacked the supposedly *unhackable* system.

This demonstrates the attacker ethos: figure out how the system is supposed to work and then make it behave differently.

HOW MINDSETS DRIVE OUTCOMES

Let's talk about injecting drugs into your spine.

After a recent security assessment of a drug infusion pump, we met with our client to review the results. We started by explaining the attack scenarios, describing how an adversary could exploit the system.

The CEO quickly interrupted, saying, "This isn't as bad as you suggest."

We paused, encouraging him to elaborate.

"Well, even though that *could* happen, that doesn't mean it's worth worrying about," he said.

Again, we encouraged him to continue.

"Let me put it this way: I drive a BMW," he said with a smile. "I love that car; I'd hate to see it scratched. Theoretically, someone could haul a piano up onto the roof of our building, throw it down onto my BMW, and destroy the car. But I'm just not worried about that."

Let that sink in for a moment.

This device injects morphine into your spine. It can literally kill you. We just showed him several ways an attacker could do exactly that. And yet, this CEO rejected the significance of security vulnerabilities that are *known to exist* in his device. Instead of fixing the problems, he tried to dismiss them.

The United States Food and Drug Administration (FDA), which approves medical devices for use on patients, did not like this CEO's minimizing attitude toward security. At first, he tried to get their approval without showing them any security assessment reports. When it became clear that the FDA wouldn't approve without seeing one, he relented and shared the report we supplied him. When they asked about his plan to remediate the issues, he shared that he didn't intend to. The device was denied approval for use on patients. Unable to sell their product, the company soon went out of business.

It's a sad story, and I certainly do not celebrate this failure. I'm an entrepreneur myself and prefer to celebrate successes! However, this cautionary tale needs to be shared. It is a powerful demonstration of how mindset dramatically impacts outcomes. They didn't want to get better, so they didn't try to get better, and so they simply didn't get better. It ended badly.

By contrast, a different client of ours *did* want to achieve security excellence. They knew that security was important to their customers, so despite their small size and limited money, they invested in manual white-box vulnerability assessments— by far the most effective approach but also the most involved (I'll explain how and why to do this).

Over the next few years, we helped them discover flaw after flaw after flaw. At times, it was unpleasant for them. Yet they kept pursuing their goal.

The engineering practices evolved. The developers got better. They stopped repeating issues. The application got stronger.

They learned how to communicate their security philosophy. They earned trust. They won sales.

Eventually, they were acquired for more than $100 million.

I'd be a fool to suggest that they were acquired only because they were secure; they obviously had the makeup of a good acquisition, including sound business fundamentals and a stellar executive team. However, they wouldn't have been in consideration if they couldn't prove security. They didn't just settle for the basics either. They sought greatness. Security excellence is what set them apart from other solutions that might have been acquired instead.

Now compare these stories side by side. One went out of business, whereas the other produced millionaires. These companies had different mindsets that led to different outcomes, but they reveal the same lesson: *How you think determines what you achieve.*

GET THE RIGHT PARTNER: EXTERNAL EXPERTISE MULTIPLIES IN-HOUSE EXPERTISE

You're not in this alone.

Security entails seemingly endless challenges, but that doesn't mean you need to be isolated in solving them. In the words of leadership author Ken Blanchard, "None of us is as smart as all of us." Teamwork is the key to your security mission.

This book assumes you engage outside experts for security testing, security consulting, or both. Whether you emphasize in-house or external expertise (or both, as I will urge you to consider), the point is the same: Find people capable of executing the ideas, strategies, and tactics in this book. Then pair them together to magnify each other's impact.

THE SKILLS SHORTAGE

However, before we can go any further, let's talk about one of the biggest constraints you'll face: *talent*. Security requires a highly specialized skillset, which is in extreme shortage and will continue to be so for the foreseeable future. There are several reasons for this skills shortage.

First, formal education isn't (yet) optimized to create enough security talent. Many ethical hackers come out of computer science degree programs, yet most programs treat security as an area of interest, rather than a core discipline. For example, programs might have an ethical hacking class or even a club, but these are not central to the degree. Security-specific degree programs are popping up, but there still aren't enough of them to produce enough skilled security professionals, let alone at the level of expertise that's needed.

Second, security requires extensive, real-world experience *outside* of the classroom. Most security degree programs teach the fundamentals, but what security professionals do in the field differs from what they learn in the classroom. Aspiring security professionals must obtain experience on *their own time* in order to prepare for the jobs that they want. Without that, it's not possible to develop into the kind of ethical hacker the world needs. At the same time, security is not a field someone can jump straight into because "entry-level" security jobs aren't really entry-level at all; they require a candidate to know computer science, networking, engineering, security principles, and even some psychology (and a lot more, too). Developing security skills takes a long time and requires accumulating deep expertise across a broad range of domains. There's no single place where all of this information can be found, so it takes a lot of grit just to *find* the relevant information, let alone *master* it.

Third, security has perception issues. Security is often perceived to be ridiculously hard, so rising computer scientists (of which ethical hackers are a subset) often pursue other things instead. This also feeds into a perception that, as one ethical hacker put it, "Security people are seen as wizards beyond mortal understanding." This suggests that if you're not already one of them, it's not worth trying to become one.

Fourth, security is adversarial. It's not just about being creative; it's about being *more* creative than someone else. Many talented people decide they'd rather compete against the constraints of what it takes to develop software than compete against other people. Most computer scientists want to build things for themselves, rather than tear apart the work of others. Yet, that's *exactly* what ethical hacking is about.

You can and should build your own expertise in-house. However, it's going to be a long, difficult road. Over the many years we've been doing this, we've yet to see a company successfully achieve their security mission with only in-house talent alone. That doesn't mean you won't be able to; it just means the odds aren't in your favor.

It's very hard to acquire the necessary skills, and not enough people have them. Sadly, people often think security is easier than it actually is. A venture capitalist once told me this about his portfolio companies: "Many entrepreneurs feel that security is an in-house competency, and young engineers are plentiful for this kind of work." I applaud his confidence but worry about the massive blind spot he doesn't realize he has. He doesn't know what you now know: there's a skills shortage and that's not changing anytime soon.

WHY YOU WANT BOTH IN-HOUSE AND EXTERNAL TEAMS

That may surprise you. You might expect it to be either one or the other, but that's not the case. Security is a team sport. External and internal expertise complement each other. They magnify each other's impact.

Your external security partner finds security vulnerabilities; you fix them. Your partner transfers knowledge; you use it to get better. Your external partner is immune to bias as well as the strong opinions of powerful leaders in your company; they just tell you how it is, even if it's not what you want to hear. You ensure the security mission is supported by executives and key stakeholders.

Together, you and your external partner reduce risk. Together, you communicate with your customers. Together, you transfer knowledge in both directions: your in-house team equips your external team with the information to make them more effective, and your external team equips your in-house team with insights about how to keep getting better. Win-win.

If you already have in-house security experts, fantastic! You're off to a good start. If you don't, that's OK, too. Your external partner serves that function right away and helps you build that capability over time.

Separation of duties is a powerful concept that you already see in other areas of your business: your chief financial officer

(CFO) works with external accountants, your general counsel works with outside law firms, and your CEO works with the board and other external advisors. It's the same idea with outside security experts; they magnify the impact made by internal resources while delivering benefits you can't get in-house.

This book helps you improve both the activities you do in-house and those you get from external partners. As we go through the ideas, I'll point out where it makes more sense for you to do it, your partner to do it, or a combination of the two.

It probably won't ever be appropriate for you to go without external expertise. Just look at the kinds of companies that hire us: Amazon, Google, Microsoft, Netflix, Adobe, and so on. Talk about enterprises that have robust in-house security teams! Yet, they nevertheless capitalize on external security expertise.

If it works for them, it will work for you, too.

BENEFITS OF IN-HOUSE EXPERTISE

First, remediation. Although you could pay your partner to fix the vulnerabilities they discover, that would probably be cost-prohibitive. Most likely, you'd want your internal resources to implement the fixes. Not only is that more cost-effective, but it also ensures that your in-house teams are intimately familiar with the problems and the solutions to those problems. As a result, your in-house teams learn from them, get better, and thus avoid making the same mistakes in the future.

Second, efficiency. Your in-house security team can deliver insights and information that makes your external team even more efficient. They set them up for success in ways that maximize your investment. They remove roadblocks, share information, and maximize outcomes. They run automated tools where appropriate, update documentation, and overall keep the projects running smoothly.

Third, consensus-building. As much as you want the unbiased opinion of outside experts, you still need someone who knows how to navigate the way things are done in your company. You need someone on the inside who truly understands the security problems at a technical level and can effectively advocate the business case for security in ways that resonate with your leadership.

BENEFITS OF EXTERNAL EXPERTISE

First and foremost, you want their specialized skills. You need both breadth (capabilities in many niches) and depth (extensive expertise in each of those niches). It's really hard to staff an internal department that delivers *all* of that. Even if you can, you wind up paying for these niche specialties even though you don't need them 100 percent of the time. However, when you hire an external partner, you get their entire team at the snap of your fingers and wind up paying for only the expertise you need, when you need it.

Second, independence. Whether you recognize it or not, there is bias in your company. Things are done a certain way. Powerful executives have strong opinions. Corporate priorities drive investment. Each of these affects how security is approached, viewed, or even talked about. These factors get in your way by inappropriately influencing approaches. That, in turn, affects outcomes. Outside experts are free from such influences. They are able to remain objective. They tell you how it is, even when it's not what you want to hear. Even though that may be uncomfortable at times, it is crucial for achieving security excellence. Independence also delivers a diversity of viewpoints, including bringing lessons learned from other companies who faced similar challenges to what you are facing.

Third, immediate impact. If you get the right kind of external partner, they'll have a variety of experts across many domains, ready to deliver impact on day one. By bringing in external expertise, you start solving your problems right away, without the long lead times to recruiting, vetting, onboarding, training, and developing talent that is required for building in-house teams.

Fourth, credibility. The ideas in this book ultimately give you a competitive edge by first improving your security and then being able to prove it. That shines in sharp contrast to the majority of companies who do neither, which, in turn, helps you earn trust and drive sales. However, your customers will likely view any security claims you make with skepticism. They know you want the sale, and assume that might influence what you will (or will not) tell them. By contrast, your customers trust the credibility and authority that comes from your independent, neutral, outside expert. Your partner of course wants you to succeed, but they won't say anything untrue (assuming they truly are independent). Your customers like that.

These conditions simply cannot be replicated internally.

HOW TO FIND THE PERFECT SECURITY PARTNER

I don't care whether you hire *my* company as your external consultants; that's not the point. I just want you to hire *a* company.

You need that external expertise. However, not all advisors are created equal. Choose carefully. To help you select the right partner, here's a rough overview of the types of security companies out there:

- **Products vs. Services**. There are three types of security companies: companies that sell only products, companies that sell only services, and companies that sell both. You can rule out companies that only sell products, as they won't be suitable as an advisor (note that almost every security program needs products, and I'm not advising you against using products. You'll need them. However, what we're talking about here is finding you an *advisor*. That, by definition, is a service, not a product). Furthermore, be leery of companies that sell both services *and* products if those services result in buying their product. For example, their consulting might inform you of a security issue that *just so happens* to be solved by a product they sell. How convenient. This directly undermines the integrity of the recommendation: is this *actually* what you need, or is this just an underhanded way to sell you their product? This is shockingly common, so beware. I'd recommend you look for a company that only sells services (or sells services and products *as long as* the products are *not* the solution to the problems the service will discover).

- **Tool-Centric vs. Human-Centric**. Your internet searches will be absolutely flooded with "service" companies that really are just running an automated tool. You can't scan your way to security excellence. Instead, you want to find an advisor who has smart, experienced experts who can help you solve your problems with the creativity that comes with being a human. The work needs to be manual.

- **Application Security vs. Other Specialties.** You're reading a book about application security, so I'm going to assume you need a company that specializes in application security (obviously, this advice would be different if you were reading a book about a different security domain). Note that some companies will present themselves as experts in *everything*. Be wary of that; no one is the expert in everything. Most companies, however, do have a specialization, even if they have a wide range of capabilities. Ask what their single strongest area is, and that should help guide you.

Once you've narrowed it down to a few potential partners, next you need to vet their capabilities. This is a classic "chicken and egg" scenario: how do you vet the qualifications of a security advisor when you need a security advisor to help you make good security decisions? I won't lie to you; it will be difficult. But here are some things to look for:

- **Security research.** The best security consulting firms all publish research that advances the state of the industry. They find vulnerabilities and disclose them to the afflicted company. They make those companies better, and they make the industry better. Look at their website to see what research they've published. If there isn't much, consider ruling them out.

- **Talks**. Usually an extension of security research, the best security professionals are out there advocating for how to do better. They're teaching insights, methods, and strategies. They're speaking at the big security industry conferences such as Black Hat or RSA Conference, the research conferences like DEF CON, or even conferences specific to your industry. Again, look at their websites. Watch a few talks to see if they seem credible to you. If they don't seem to be giving many talks, consider ruling them out.

- **Methodology**. The best will work in close collaboration with you, rather than operating closed off from you. They know who the attackers are, how they think, and how they operate. This is precisely the mindset you need in order to find and fix your most serious security vulnerabilities. Probe to understand their methodology, and make sure that it echoes these ideas. We'll thoroughly explore methodology in chapter 2.

- **Deliverables**. The best companies equip you with the reports and documents that you need in order to both reduce risk and earn trust. They give you clarity on the issues found, how severe they are, and what to do about them. If it seems like the deliverable will be an enormous list of scan results without any false positives removed, you're probably not talking to the right partner; you're probably talking to someone who uses a tool-based approach. By contrast, if it looks like the reports and other deliverables will give you the precise plan, simplified so as to be actionable and prioritized by criticality, then you're probably on the right track. In chapter 3, I'll further explain how to analyze a report to make sure it's giving you what you need.

Look for these traits, and you'll find a partner who can help you achieve security excellence.

Security is like fitness, and external security experts are like your personal trainers. Although it's ultimately up to you whether you'll achieve your fitness goals, your likelihood of success skyrockets when you bring the right attitude and have the right fitness expert helping you. They apply years of experience. They point out where your form is bad and help you fix it. They hold you accountable. They make you better.

That's exactly what security is like, too.

How you think determines what you achieve: pair in-house experts with external experts as you pursue security excellence. Together, these things are the foundation of everything this book delivers for you. With them, you *will* achieve your security mission.

BIG IDEAS

Security starts with the right mindset, combined with the right partnership.

- Security excellence is the relentless pursuit of *better*. It's about constant improvement. Strive not just to build good products but to build *secure* products. Recognize that this work is never done.

- To defend against attackers, you need to think like them. Figure out how the system is supposed to work, and then make it behave differently.

- How you think determines what you achieve.

- Security requires a highly specialized skillset, which is in extreme shortage and will continue to be so for the foreseeable future.

- Build in-house capabilities *and* partner with external experts. They complement each other and magnify each other's impact. In-house teams and external partners play different but complementary roles.

- You want in-house experts because they perform remediations cost-effectively, they make your external partner more efficient, and they know how to build consensus within your company.

- You want external advisors to deliver specialized skills, independence, credibility, and immediate impact.

- Not all security companies are the same, so understand the differences and pick an advisor that will help you achieve your goals.

For downloadable templates, team exercises, and real-world examples, go to *tedharrington.com/hackable.*

Now that you've established the foundation that leads to success, you need to choose the most effective methodology. Black-box limits information and thus limits value, whereas white-box maximizes information and thus maximizes value.

CHAPTER 2

CHOOSE THE RIGHT ASSESSMENT METHODOLOGY

LIE
*Withholding information from my security
assessors gets me "real-world results."*

TRUTH
I need to give info to get value.

U nfortunately for a medieval king, pretty much everybody wanted to kill him pretty much all of the time.

Imagine a castle. Let's pretend that the king wants to know if he could be assassinated. He orders a loyal noble to send some knights to try to break into the castle. He gives no information to those knights about the castle defenses. After all, the king thinks that what he needs is for them to pretend to be his enemies, and his enemies don't have any of that information.

The knights are given a limited amount of time to attack the castle. They find a few weaknesses in the castle defenses, some of which the king already knew about and some he didn't. Ultimately, they determine they cannot assassinate the king.

A few weeks later, the king is murdered. His enemies found a secret tunnel that the knights didn't know about and used it to get to the king. The king knew about this secret tunnel; it was his escape route in the event of a siege. But he never told the knights about it.

The king represents your assets.

The castle represents your defenses.

The knights represent your security evaluators.

This is what black-box testing is like. When the king withholds information that would help the knights do their jobs, he reduces their ability to help him. Security testing that's done with a black-box methodology intentionally limits information. All that does is limit *value*. Instead, you want to share information in order to maximize value. The less information you share with your external security partner, the less value you get. The more information you share with your external security partner, the more value you get.

Get white-box, not black-box.

BLACK-BOX VS. WHITE-BOX

Now that you've figured out *whom* to work with, you need to figure out *how* to work with them. There are two approaches: black-box or white-box. Black-box is a security-testing methodology that limits information in a (flawed) attempt to replicate real-world conditions. White-box is a security-testing methodology that maximizes information sharing in order to amplify the value of the assessment. Many people mistakenly seek out black-box, but what you want to do is pursue white-box instead.

In black-box, you don't tell your security evaluators anything about how the system works. You don't share diagrams or documentation. You don't allow them to glean insights from your engineers. In white-box, you provide all of those things instead.

This all comes down to *information*. Attackers have all the time in the world to attack. Yet, your available resources to defend against them are limited. You need to squeeze every advantage you can just to keep up. Information is one such advantage. You have it, and your attackers don't.

Limiting the supply of information is counterproductive. But it happens all the time because people mistakenly believe this approach somehow delivers "real-world results." It does not do that. Instead, it causes these three bad things to happen.

BLACK-BOX FLAW #1: YOU WASTE TIME AND MONEY

The knights spent time figuring out how deep the moat was, how many alligators were in it, and where it would be easiest to cross. The king already knew all of these things. Every minute the knights spent trying to figure them out didn't help the king.

A black-box assessment limits the information supplied to your assessor. The only thing this does is require them to invest time—your time and your money—in obtaining information you could supply in minutes. You literally pay them to figure out the things you already know. Worse yet, it rarely results in the same level of knowledge that would be delivered if you just told them.

BLACK-BOX FLAW #2:
YOU DON'T TEST YOUR SYSTEM;
YOU TEST YOUR PARTNER

The king determined that these particular knights didn't break in, but that didn't mean that other knights—let alone his enemies—couldn't. What had he actually evaluated? The *knights*, not his *defenses*.

The sneakiest drawback to black-box testing is that you aren't testing the *system*; you're testing your *partner*. In black-box, you literally determine whether *this* security expert can compromise *this* system within *this* amount of effort.

Yes, you absolutely must vet the skills of your security partner. You should only work with experts skilled enough to solve your problems. No question. But you want to figure that out *before* you start testing; it should not be the *purpose* of your testing. You hire them to test *you*, not to test *them*. If you need to validate the skills of your assessors, there are better and less expensive ways to do that.

Security is about finding and fixing flaws. However, black-box methodology is about limiting information, which limits value.

BLACK-BOX FLAW #3: YOU GET
LOW-VALUE RESULTS

When you limit information, it limits value in three nasty ways:

1. **If vulnerabilities aren't found, it does not mean they don't exist.** In black-box testing, your security evaluators don't know how the system works. If they do not find

vulnerabilities, you cannot assume it's because none exist. The lack of findings doesn't mean lack of issues; it simply means nothing was found yet. You have no way of knowing if there are other issues or even how close to discovering an issue they may have been. Security is about understanding and minimizing risk. A black-box methodology does not help you with either.

2. **If *some* vulnerabilities are found, it doesn't mean *all* of them were found.** Is what you found comprehensive or just scratching the surface? How much attack surface—the points where data is transferred or accessed—did you actually cover? With an incomplete understanding of vulnerabilities, how do you know where to invest time, money, and effort to fix issues? This problem is magnified by the false sense of calm it delivers. You might learn about some vulnerabilities, assume they entail everything important, and blindly focus on just fixing those issues. Yet, there may be plenty of other issues you don't know about, including more severe issues. Security is about being able to prioritize risk. Black-box testing delivers incomplete results that do not empower you to prioritize risk.

3. **You don't get helpful remediations.** In black-box testing, your partners don't know how the system works, so they can't recommend how to fix any issues they find. This handcuffs you. You might be able to figure out the solution on your own. However, (a) it puts the onus back on you to do the problem-solving, (b) you lose the many years of experience that your security partner has with solving problems just like yours, which means that (c) you get less value out of what you're paying for. Security is about fixing issues in order to get better. A black-box methodology does a poor job of equipping you to fix the issues.

WHY WHITE-BOX IS BETTER

Imagine instead that the king walks the knights around the castle, pointing out the features of the walls, moats, and turrets. He has the knights speak directly with the guards themselves and review the blueprints with the castle architect. As a result, the knights intimately understand the castle defenses and can probe accordingly for weaknesses.

That's what white-box testing is like. In white-box, you collaborate closely with your security partner. You provide information that makes them faster, more efficient, and more effective. They review design documents, work with your engineers, and analyze source code. You treat them as part of your team. You show them how the system works. You explain workflows, access provisioning, user onboarding, and the future development roadmap.

Perhaps most importantly, you explain your business. You teach about your customers, what matters, and why. By understanding the business, your security partner knows how to think about your technology. It helps them understand your security vulnerabilities in the proper context. By understanding your mission, they help you secure it. White-box is about collaboration. Collaboration delivers value. Here's why.

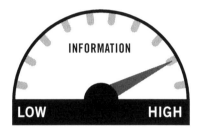 

WHITE-BOX ADVANTAGE #1: YOU MAKE THE BEST USE OF YOUR TIME AND MONEY

If the king explained his defenses, the knights wouldn't need to spend time figuring them out. They wouldn't need to count alligators; they could just know how many there are and spend time probing for weaknesses instead. Rather than spending whole days or weeks documenting the castle guard's routes and schedules, the knights could just be given that info up front to analyze.

A white-box methodology accelerates the timeline to receiving value. Your enemy has endless time to gather information, but you don't. You want the testing effort focused on using the information, rather than on finding the information. When you supply information, you get a shortcut that your enemy doesn't have. This helps skilled security professionals quickly zoom in on where the problems might be and then probe from there. Further, because they know how the system works, they can examine issues that might never be found in black-box testing.

WHITE-BOX ADVANTAGE #2: YOU CAN MAKE DECISIONS CONFIDENTLY

At its core, the king summoned those knights because he wanted to sleep with confidence. A white-box methodology is the best way to achieve it.

White-box is about receiving information, too; the more you have, the more confidently you make decisions. If security vulnerabilities are found, you'll know that they entail most (or maybe even all!) that exist. Conversely, if none are found, you can be reasonably confident that few exist. You can confidently communicate risk to your board, customers, shareholders, and employees. A white-box methodology delivers all of these, whereas black-box delivers none. Keep in mind, however, that you only find vulnerabilities within the assessment scope. You won't find anything where you don't look. Yet, it's very common for people to cut investment, which cuts effort, which forces some elements of the attack surface out of scope. You'll learn more about this problem in chapter 7.

White-box testing helps you solve security problems in ways that advance—rather than hinder—your business. A security flaw that affects core business functionality is much more severe than one that doesn't. By accounting for technical issues in the context of how they relate to the business, you resolve vulnerabilities in ways that support your company's mission. All of this empowers you to make good, well-informed business decisions.

Security is about achieving confidence. White-box is the best methodology to obtain it.

WHITE-BOX ADVANTAGE #3: YOU GET BETTER

If the knights had found the tunnel, they could have helped the king understand why it was a vulnerability. This creates the opportunity to get better. Consider how a monarch is protected today compared to medieval times. Enormous advancements in technology, strategy, and tactics mean that a king is much safer from assassination attempts now. Relentlessly trying to get better is what drives those advancements.

You are the kind of person who is reading a book about achieving excellence, so it's a safe bet that you're trying to get better, too. A white-box methodology helps you not only find security vulnerabilities but also understand them and learn how to fix them. These insights help you evolve so you can avoid similar vulnerabilities in the future. They help developers enhance their skills. They transfer knowledge from your security partner to your in-house teams. They help you get better.

It's possible that you could get better with a black-box assessment, too, but the burden is much higher on you, involves a lot of guesswork, and in the process, you lose much of your security partner's expertise.

Security is about finding vulnerabilities, fixing them, and adapting. These ultimately make you better. A white-box methodology is the best way to do that.

WHY WOULD ANYONE CHOOSE BLACK-BOX?

When it comes to the mission of finding and fixing your security vulnerabilities, white-box delivers far superior outcomes than black-box does. However, there are some cases where black-box is usually unavoidable.

First, when dependencies are involved. Applications commonly integrate with other technologies, such as third-party libraries, shared components, or other aspects of the supply chain.[11] Whenever the scope includes another company's technology, any testing on those components will almost certainly be done black-box (unless you can convince that other company to share sensitive, proprietary information about how their technology works. Good luck with that).

Second, when it's security research. This is almost always done black-box because the company being researched usually doesn't know it's happening. Even when they do know, they usually don't want to participate or share information. In either case, black-box is usually the only way forward.

Third, when the goal is to test for reconnaissance rather than for vulnerabilities. If you want to evaluate how easy it is for attackers to gather information, that's a valid thing to test via black-box. You'd identify processes that leak information and, as a result, improve them. However, for all of the reasons mentioned in this chapter, it's not a good way to find vulnerabilities, let alone fix them.

---

11 Integrations are a delicious target for attackers, so make sure you're considering them. We'll get to this when we talk about attack surfaces in chapter 8.

Security is an uphill battle. You're outmatched by motivated adversaries who have more time, money, and resources than you do. You need to squeeze maximum efficiency out of your investment. White-box is the best way to do that.

CASE STUDY: BLACK-BOX VS. WHITE-BOX

Here's an example of this contrast playing out in real life.

A client of ours wanted to test their newest application for security vulnerabilities. For years, they'd only ever asked us for white-box testing, but this time they asked for black-box.

Surprised, I asked their director of product security why.

"First of all," he said, "I definitely want white-box—I desperately need to know what security vulnerabilities exist so I can fix them." He explained, "But *my* boss promised a black-box test to *his* boss who then promised it to *her* boss. They didn't understand the difference, but nevertheless, I must deliver it. It's political now." This was quite the conundrum and one that commonly plays out in many companies. (Does this sound like your company, too, where business decisions drive bad security decisions? If so, you're not alone.)

Together, we developed a plan: do both.

On the same system, we performed two security assessments: one black-box and then one white-box. This satisfied both the technical need and the political need, but it also delivered something else: a side-by-side comparison of outcomes. (If you're wondering how the director of product security came up with funding for two assessments: he made a compelling case for why they needed the side-by-side comparison to inform future decisions. His finance department agreed.)

Here's what happened.

First, we performed the black-box assessment. We allocated 200 person-hours and found four security vulnerabilities as a result. Of those, our client already knew about two of them. All of the time and effort invested in discovering these delivered zero value to the customer. The third issue turned out not to be a vulnerability after all but rather a misunderstanding. Remember: in black-box testing, information is intentionally withheld, which led to a misinterpretation of why certain inputs produced certain outputs. Because it was not actually a security vulnerability at all, this too was of no value to the customer. The fourth vulnerability was indeed a previously unknown, critical security vulnerability. This was very valuable to our customer. However, we couldn't recommend how to fix it because we didn't know how the system worked.

In summary, this was the outcome of the black-box assessment:

200 person-hours = 1 vulnerability and 0 fixes

Next, we performed the white-box assessment. Like the black-box assessment, we allocated the same 200 person-hours. Unlike the black-box assessment, where we found only one security vulnerability, in the white-box assessment, we found twenty-one.

Let that sink in.

Twenty-one important issues instead of just one!

All of them were previously unknown, critical security vulnerabilities. This was enormously valuable to the customer! All of these issues existed in the system while we did the black-box assessment; we just didn't find them within the allotted time.

Such is the power of information. For every single issue, we could recommend at least one remediation and, in some cases, more than one. Because information is provided in white-box, you equip your partner to recommend remediations for any vulnerabilities found. This, too, was enormously valuable to the customer.

In summary, this was the outcome of the white-box assessment:

$$200\ person\text{-}hours = 21\ vulnerabilities\ and\ 21+\ fixes$$

Same effort.

Same system.

Different methodologies.

Dramatically different outcomes.

This data overwhelmingly makes the point: *methodology matters.*

When the director of product security received this comparison, his eyes grew as wide as dinner plates. He literally shouted, "We're never going black-box again!" And he hasn't.

The metaphorical king lost his life because he didn't understand the difference between methodologies, but now you do. Implement these ideas, and you'll be able to better protect your most valuable assets.

BIG IDEAS

Get white-box, not black-box.

- Black-box is a security-testing methodology that limits information in a (flawed) attempt to replicate real-world conditions. White-box is a security-testing methodology that maximizes information sharing in order to amplify the value of the assessment. Many people mistakenly seek out black-box, but what you want to do is pursue white-box instead.

- Avoid black-box methodology because you:
  - Waste time and money
  - Test your partner, not your system
  - Get low-value results

- Get white-box methodology because you:
  - Make the best use of your time and money
  - Make decisions confidently
  - Get better

- Methodology matters. White-box testing is exponentially more effective than black-box at helping you identify and remediate security risks.

For downloadable templates, team exercises, and real-world examples, go to *tedharrington.com/hackable*.

Now that you've learned the distinction between testing methodologies, let's distinguish the different types. You're probably asking for penetration testing but being sold vulnerability scanning. Yet, what you need are vulnerability assessments.

CHAPTER 3

GET THE RIGHT SECURITY TESTING

LIE

I need "penetration testing."

TRUTH

That term might not mean what I think it means.

You may be doing it wrong.

But hopefully, you're just *talking* about it wrong.

When it comes to testing applications for security vulnerabilities, terms are used incorrectly all the time. If you don't realize it's happening, it can have dire consequences.

Pretend that your cat is sick. You call the veterinarian, explain the symptoms, and the vet gives you advice. However, your cat doesn't get better. So you bring your cat to the vet's office. When she asks to see the cat, she's met with a surprise: it's not a cat, it's a horse.

That's why the treatment wasn't working: a cat and a horse are not the same thing. They require different treatments.

Cat   Not a Cat

Yes, this metaphor is ridiculous. But there's truth in absurdity. *Words matter.* When talking about security, people are often as ridiculous as saying "cat" when they mean "horse."

Different security terms mean different things, yet they're often used interchangeably. They should not be. They're different things!

You may not even realize this problem exists. It's hard to tell the difference, but it's important that you do. Otherwise, you might invest in security that doesn't meet your goals.

Security terms are not interchangeable. If you use the wrong term, you get the wrong thing. Make sure you get the right thing.

THEY'RE NOT THE SAME THING!

"Security assessment" is an umbrella term for all varieties of security testing. The most commonly referenced one is "penetration testing." That has become a catchall term. Unfortunately, it's misleading.

True penetration testing is a tactical service suitable only for robust, hardened, thoroughly tested systems. However, when you ask for "penetration testing," many providers tend to deliver something else entirely: lightweight vulnerability scanning. And if you weren't already frustrated enough, there's this: what you actually need is usually something completely different from either of those things. You probably need manual, white-box, vulnerability assessments.

Pause and think about that.

You ask for penetration testing.

You're sold vulnerability scanning.

But what you actually need are vulnerability assessments.

What you're asking for	What you're being sold	What you actually need
PENETRATION TESTING*	**VULNERABILITY SCANNING**	**VULNERABILITY ASSESSMENTS**

* Only suitable for robust, thoroughly tested systems.

Those are three exceedingly different things. Each entails different approaches, levels of effort, cost, and outcomes.

Your security struggles are hard enough as it is. The last thing you need is to get the wrong outcomes simply because terms got mixed up. The marketing nonsense has gotten so bad that it's challenging to distinguish what's what. The reason for this is simple: proper penetration testing is badass! It pits a skilled expert against your defenses in a win-or-die mission to see if you're secure. Any marketer would want their security service to sound like that! Unfortunately, it's also very hard to do (and isn't even appropriate for most systems anyway). As you learned earlier, there's a skills shortage, so there simply aren't enough people with enough expertise to do this properly. So what naturally happens is that other approaches—those driven largely by tools instead of experts—simply adopt the terminology. The marketing logic is pretty straightforward: if it sounds like the service people want, then people will probably buy it.

This term confusion is so widespread that regulatory bodies and even your customers may explicitly require "penetration testing," which drives you to seek that specific service by name. But, of course, they're usually misusing the term, too. What they really want is to ensure you have solid security and continue to improve it (as you'd get with vulnerability assessments). They're usually not looking for something that just scratches the surface (as you'd get when your "penetration testing" winds up being just vulnerability scanning instead). Yet, they're unwittingly directing you with the wrong terms.

The deck is unfairly stacked against you. There are lots of attackers, attack surfaces, and unknown vulnerabilities, and the very services that address this chaos are themselves unclear.

That's a lot to deal with.

If you want to have a chance at finding and fixing your vulnerabilities, defending against attackers, and proving that your app is secure, you absolutely must distinguish these terms. That's how you make sure that you get the testing you need. Because it's not the *term* that matters; it's the *outcome*.

WHAT IS PENETRATION TESTING ANYWAY?

Penetration testing seeks a binary outcome: did you or did you not achieve a specific end result?

Yes or no. That's it.

Often referred to as a "pen test" or sometimes "red teaming" (which is actually something different; red teaming tests your security team's response capabilities), penetration testing is a time-constrained effort to measure a single outcome. For example, a penetration test might seek to determine "could an attacker escalate basic user privileges to admin rights?" The outcome is either yes or no. There is no other outcome.

Penetration testing is like a crash test. When auto manufacturers want to understand the safety implications of a specific situation (such as a frontal collision), they run a crash simulation. They literally crash the car into a wall to see what happens. As a result, they have a clear answer about how the system performs in that specific situation.

Penetration testing is about depth in a specific area. It usually focuses on known classes of vulnerabilities rather than on finding new zero-days (the type of catastrophic vulnerability that you have literally zero days to fix because it's exploitable in the wild right now). However, when you say you want "penetration testing," there's a good chance you're actually looking for something else: you need to learn what you don't know, find vulnerabilities across many attack surfaces, understand how severe they are, and fix them. Penetration testing is not designed to do that.

Let's use your house as a metaphor. Let's pretend you have a valuable diamond ring to protect.

The house represents your app.

The security measures, such as doors and locks, represent your defenses.

The diamond ring represents the assets your app protects, such as sensitive data.

In a penetration test, you would seek to answer the question: could a thief steal the ring?

Let's say the thief sees the ring on your kitchen counter, breaks a window, and grabs the ring. This would be a successful penetration test: it delivered a clear yes to the binary question of whether a thief could steal the ring.

But what has this informed you about your security overall? What have you learned about the locks on the front door, the surveillance system, or the second-floor windows?

Nothing.

Because that's not the point of a penetration test.

The point of a penetration test is not to find and fix as many issues as possible; it is to evaluate a specific outcome. It seeks a simple yes or no.

Penetration testing is great when you have a mature, robust, well-tested defense, and you want to determine if that defense still stands up to a simulated attack. It's appropriate after you've invested heavily in vulnerability assessments, code reviews, and other security testing. It's a reality check, performed periodically, to measure how you're progressing in your relentless pursuit of becoming secure.

WHEN "PENETRATION TESTING" IS REALLY JUST VULNERABILITY SCANNING

You just learned what penetration testing is *supposed* to be. Unfortunately, the term is often used for something remarkably different. Often, when you ask for penetration testing, you'll be sold vulnerability scanning instead. Your search results on Google will be absolutely flooded with this inappropriate use of the term. Thanks to misleading marketing and confused customers, "vulnerability scanning" has become synonymous with "penetration testing."

It's not.

Vulnerability scanning is running an automated tool that looks for common vulnerabilities that are known to exist. The goal is to quickly and inexpensively find basic issues, including checking for unpatched vulnerabilities. Given that running a scanner is one of the first steps your attacker will take, it's a good idea for you to do this, too. You want to see what they see.

It's like the diagnostic tool that mechanics use when the "check engine" light comes on in your car. The tool scans for known issues, spitting back readable codes. It's easy, inexpensive, and quick. However, it may report false positives, and the codes don't always tell you what the root cause is. This isn't a comprehensive way to evaluate vehicle safety.

Here's what's crazy about the term confusion surrounding penetration testing: even if you didn't realize it, you technically asked to crash-test your car, but then you were sold a diagnostic scan of what's causing the "check engine" light. Those things are pretty different! Sometimes it's easy to tell the difference in service descriptions; the method will literally describe an automated scan. Other times, it's not obvious because the method will mention a manual component, but that only references the work done to remove false positives. Sometimes descriptions are even intentionally misleading. If you're unsure how to tell the difference between what you need and what's being sold, here are a few ways to sniff out the difference:

- **Price**. Vulnerability scanning usually costs around 10–20 percent of vulnerability assessments (which we'll discuss in a moment). Not 20 percent *less*, 20 percent *of* (or said another way: 80 percent less). Two dollars instead of ten dollars.

- **Timeline**. Vulnerability scanning is usually done in a few days rather than the weeks that vulnerability assessments require.

Vulnerability scanning is great when you need to find common vulnerabilities or find unpatched vulnerabilities. It's great for gathering information to use in a broader security assessment. It's good when you need to keep timelines, effort, or cost to an absolute minimum (with the understanding that these tradeoffs also limit the value of what you get as a result).

Vulnerability scanning has some drawbacks, though. It reports false positives. That's confusing and creates unnecessary work for you. Vulnerability scanning does assign severity ratings, but they're not calibrated to your context and circumstances. It doesn't account for your threat model, nor does a threat model even matter when running a tool (we'll discuss threat modeling in chapter 8).

Depending on your business, a given vulnerability might be significantly more severe or significantly less severe than the one-size-fits-all definitions used by tools. Remediation guidance is either vague (and thus difficult to implement) or outright omitted (and thus a burden on you to figure out how to fix the issues). Scan results are not calibrated to your risk appetite. Scanning doesn't provide insight into areas that are not quite exploitable but should be improved anyway.

Vulnerability scanning doesn't test access controls between the system's custom roles and permissions, leaving an important security consideration unchecked. Most importantly, scanning can only look for predefined issues and cannot find custom exploits (attacks that are unique to the way your technology is designed and implemented). It can only find common issues that are known to exist.

Finally, vulnerability scanners are inconsistent. For example, we recently wanted to evaluate some scanners, so we programmed an application to be vulnerable and ran several scanners against it to see how they'd perform. Some worked as promised, but most failed to find all of the basic vulnerabilities. Some even missed entire *classes* of vulnerabilities. It's incorrect to assume that every scanner will catch everything (including even every basic thing).

In the home robbery metaphor, vulnerability scanning is like the thief walking up to your front door and trying the handle. He knows that many people don't lock their doors, so he's checking to see if you locked yours. And that's about it. He wouldn't try to pick your lock, guess your garage keypad combination, or determine how to get onto your roof and enter through a skylight. He certainly couldn't tell you anything about the security measures inside the house.

Think of it this way: Tools are useful and should be part of your strategy. Tools should not be your *entire* strategy.

You must go past the basics to find your most important vulnerabilities. The zero-days, custom exploits, and unknown unknowns (flaws so unexpected you don't even consider them) all require a higher level of effort and expertise. They require intuition, manual investigation, and an attacker mindset. You want real humans reviewing your code and hacking your system.

You can't get these with vulnerability scanning. You get all of them with vulnerability assessments.

WHY YOU (PROBABLY) NEED
VULNERABILITY ASSESSMENTS INSTEAD

Vulnerability assessments are comprehensive, rigorous, manual efforts to discover security vulnerabilities, assign severity ratings to them, and determine how to fix them. The objective is to find as many as possible and remediate them. As a result, you understand and reduce risk.

Vulnerability assessments consider assets, attackers, attack surfaces, workflows, whole system configuration, and your future development roadmap. They adopt an attacker's perspective to look for both common vulnerabilities and custom exploits. They consider your business itself because vulnerability severity is influenced by factors such as who uses the app and how you make money.

Vulnerability assessments leverage experienced humans who solve problems manually in order to address your unique circumstances. In the real world, you're defending against smart, motivated, problem-solving humans—not just scans. Vulnerability assessments help you defend accordingly.

Vulnerability assessments go for breadth. Instead of a single crash test or a quick diagnostic scan of your car, it's more like automotive safety engineering: a complete review where testing looks for all possible faults in all safety systems, from seat belts to airbags to driver-assisted braking—and how all those systems work together. Then a report is compiled with all findings quantified and ranked by criticality. A plan is outlined for how to fix each flaw in order to improve overall vehicle safety.

Vulnerability assessments are great for both well-hardened systems as well as those still figuring it out (and everyone in between). They are the most effective way to reduce the likelihood that a real-world attacker can exploit your system.

Let's revisit the house metaphor: unlike a penetration test (where any single exploit scenario marks the test as successful) or a vulnerability scan (where only the obvious basics are investigated), in a vulnerability assessment, you'd investigate *all* of the different ways a thief could break into your house.

You contemplate the motivations and skill levels of different thieves. You examine how your family accesses your house. You consider which contractors, cleaners, or neighbors have keys. You study your fences, alarms, locks, cameras, and safes, probing your assumptions about how these work together. As a result, you identify the issues you need to worry about. You prioritize them, determining changes you need to make in order to better protect the diamond ring.

If you're currently doing security testing, but you're not sure whether it's vulnerability scanning or vulnerability assessments, just look at the reports you're getting. You can see a glaring difference.

	Vulnerability Scan Reports	Vulnerability Assessment Reports
False Positives	Remain. This adds confusion and effort, as you have to verify if the issue is legitimate.	Removed. This simplifies things for you, as you can focus just on the items that need attention.
Duplicate Issues	The same issue is noted every time, adding bulk and bloat to the report.	Unique instances of issues are reported, with repeated issues consolidated. This makes it easier for you to understand what to fix, how to fix it, and what to prioritize.

	Vulnerability Scan Reports	Vulnerability Assessment Reports
Severity Tailoring (*We'll explore severity ratings in chapter 5*)	Severity is not calibrated to your unique scenario, minimizing the value of this information.	Severity is calibrated to your unique scenario, helping you prioritize.
Threat Model (*We'll explore threat modeling in chapter 8*)	Not accounted for. This leaves you to figure out how to interpret the results in the context of your business.	Accounted for. This helps you think strategically about how the issues impact your unique situation.
Remediations (*We'll explore remediations in chapter 5*)	Vague if included, or sometimes not included at all, making it difficult to fix any discovered issues.	Tells you how to fix any discovered issues, tailored to your technology stack.
Hardening Guidance	Does not advise about improving areas that aren't quite exploitable but should be improved anyway.	Advises how to improve even areas that aren't quite exploitable.
Risk Appetite (*We'll explore risk in chapter 7*)	Does not account for your risk appetite, making it harder to know what to do with the results.	Accounts for your risk appetite, making it easier to know what to do with the results.
Vulnerability Types (*We'll explore this in chapter 4*)	Can find only predetermined vulnerabilities that it knows to look for.	Entails creative problem-solving by humans that can chain exploits, apply new techniques, and find custom exploits.

	Vulnerability Scan Reports	Vulnerability Assessment Reports
Evaluation of Permissions Model	Does not test access controls between the system's custom roles and permissions, leaving an important security consideration unchecked.	Considers access controls between the system's custom roles and permissions and how an attacker might abuse those controls.

The beauty of vulnerability assessments is that although they require time, effort, and resources, they produce valuable outcomes as a result. They help you find and fix issues. They help you get better.

WHAT TO DO WHEN YOU'RE "NOT READY"

It's fairly common to hear people say, "We're not ready. I know you'll find vulnerabilities." As a result, they delay security assessments because they think it would be a waste of money to pay someone to tell them things they already know. I empathize with that concern; everyone wants to be smart about how to spend their limited resources, especially time and money. The good news, though, is that you can get the help you need without wasting those resources. The solution is simple: just tell your security partner about the issues you're aware of! They'll include those in the context of their recommendations but focus their effort on other things. As a result, you'll get the remediation plan you need without wasting time, money, or effort on the things you already know about. (Remember: you want to do white-box testing. This is a great example of why.)

You want to avoid the unpleasant side effect of the "we're not ready" concern: when you delay security, you delay getting better. You allow issues to linger. You remain vulnerable longer than you should. Instead, *just get started*. That keeps you on the path to security excellence. You'll always have some degree of vulnerabilities to address, and your security partner should be able to help you address them *and* get value out of your investment (assuming you chose the right partner). Don't let the fact that you *know* about security issues be the reason you don't *fix* them!

The whole point of the vulnerability assessment is to help you fix your security issues and improve development practices. That's a good thing, not a bad thing. You want to do something about your vulnerabilities.

CASE STUDY: A VULNERABILITY ASSESSMENT IN ACTION

A cryptocurrency developer asked us to evaluate their trading platform, a system that stores a user's digital currency. A system like this has two components worth noting: (a) the web application to manage your funds and (b) the blockchain, which is the distributed ledger of transactions. The web app requires a username and password like most applications, and the blockchain

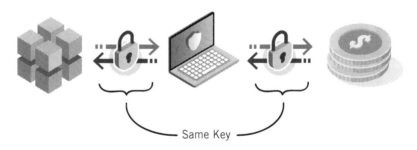
Same Key

requires a private key to register transactions. These should be different credentials. However, for the sake of user convenience, the system was designed to use the same credentials for both.

We discovered an authorization flaw where the system failed to prevent any single user from enumerating all other users. If an attacker creates an account, she can identify every other account. Cryptocurrency wallets are designed to allow offline use. So equipped with the complete list of users, an attacker can then perform an offline brute-force attack. Due to being offline, rate-limiting protections don't work, thereby allowing unlimited attempts to crack the wallet password. With enough computational power, it will be broken within minutes. With the wallet password in hand, the attacker now also has the web app's password, because they're the same. The attacker then logs into the web app and transfers all currency into the attacker's account and then repeats the attack for every account across the system. The result is a complete system compromise.

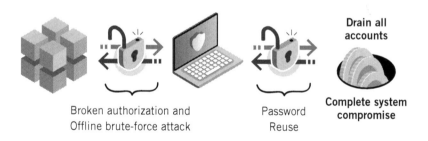

Broken authorization and
Offline brute-force attack

Password
Reuse

Drain all
accounts

**Complete system
compromise**

This could never be discovered by a tool. That's why vulnerability scanning alone is insufficient. Penetration testing could arrive at this outcome, but that would be the end of the testing; with penetration testing, there's no need to look for other vulnerabilities once the effort is successful. However, plenty of other serious vulnerabilities existed, including traffic in plaintext, confidential info sent to third parties, weak password hashing, unauthenticated API calls, and overly privileged cloud platform permissions, just to name a few.[12] Make no doubt: the customer wanted to know about and fix those, too. In vulnerability assessments, all of these were identified, rated by severity, and assigned a remediation plan.

That's why you want vulnerability assessments. You obtain a comprehensive understanding of your issues so you can fix them.

A QUICK NOTE ABOUT BUG BOUNTY PROGRAMS

A discussion of security testing would be incomplete without mentioning bug bounty programs. They are formalized crowdsourcing initiatives that reward security researchers for finding flaws in a company's technology. In contrast to hiring a dedicated company for security testing, bug bounty programs are designed to encourage a broad pool of individual researchers all over the world to come to you. Bug bounty programs are in *addition* to security testing that you engage directly with a security expert. They're not a *replacement*.

Let me repeat that: *bug bounty programs do not replace direct engagement of security testing.*

However, that's exactly what many companies try to do with them.

Bug bounty programs deliver some powerful benefits. You can work with researchers all over the world, avoiding border

12 For the sake of brevity, it's not important to define each of these; just know that they are bad.

restrictions or visa requirements. You get instant return on investment (ROI) because you only pay when valid vulnerabilities are reported. You get a great marketing tool by being able to publicly demonstrate your security approach. In *theory*, you get testing done by lots of researchers and get more eyes on your system.

However, there are big drawbacks. Bug bounty programs don't guarantee that enough people will actually look at your system. They don't guarantee that researchers with high levels of skill will participate. Results are commonly of low quality. These programs are usually operated mostly black-box, so you incur all of the drawbacks of withholding information that you learned about in the last chapter. You miss out on knowledge transfer because there is only minimal collaboration with the researcher, and as a result, you're likely to keep paying over and over for the same symptom without addressing the root cause.

Furthermore, these programs tend to be unappealing to some of the more talented security researchers. Payments are small. Valid submissions are commonly refused payment. The work is done entirely at risk without any guarantee of finding issues or making any money. By participating, researchers are prohibited from publishing research or giving talks about it—even if the bug bounty program refuses payment. When that happens, the researcher is left with no compensation (in terms of either money or public recognition) for the time and effort invested in finding the vulnerability. Unfortunately, that happens frequently, which is hugely disincentivizing and drives many talented researchers away from these programs.

Finally, be wary of the incentive mismatch: the bounties paid by the sponsoring company are usually relatively small, whereas information about zero-day vulnerabilities can command enormous sums on the black market. For example, in 2020, a vulnerability in the Zoom video conferencing platform was on sale for $500,000.[13] Bug bounty programs typically pay out less than 0.5 percent of that. Don't forget that bug bounty programs are designed to attract people who want to make money from your vulnerabilities. If their ethics are squishy, your vulnerability could make them a lot more money on the black market.

Here's a way to think about how bug bounty programs fit into your overall testing strategy. When something ails you, you go to your doctor. You tell her everything you can. You work directly with your doctor and her medical staff, and they're all at your service. You tell them your symptoms, and they ask lots of questions. They diagnose your issues, give you a treatment plan, and you get better. You have their dedicated attention. You can verify that they're qualified. That's what it's like to engage directly with a security firm doing white-box vulnerability assessments. By contrast, a bug bounty program would be like posting your symptoms on the internet and asking for advice. In theory, you'd get advice from people all over the world for a very low cost (or even free). You'd get some good advice (and a lot of bad advice). And you'd have difficulty vetting the qualifications of the people who give you that advice.

You'd never, ever, *ever* rely on the internet alone to guide your medical treatment. You'd work directly with your doctor. Maybe

---

13 Lorenzo Franceschi-Bicchiera, "Hackers Are Selling a Critical Zoom Zero-Day Exploit for $500,000," *Motherboard*, April 15, 2020, https://www.vice.com/en_us/article/qjdqgv/hackers-selling-critical-zoom-zero-day-exploit-for-500000.

you'd see a doctor *and* post to the internet. But you'd never rely on just the internet.

Same idea with your security testing. You can do just vulnerability assessments, or you can do both vulnerability assessments combined with a bug bounty program. You should *not* do just a bug bounty program alone.

However, be wary of bug bounty programs that encourage exactly that, positioning themselves to look like substitutes for vulnerability assessments. They're still done through crowdsourcing, with all of the same drawbacks already mentioned.

On the bright side, the drawbacks of bug bounty programs are mostly neutralized when paired with your existing vulnerability assessment program. This enables you to get the best of both worlds. You get the optics, ROI, and reach benefits of the bug bounty program, and you get the dedicated, thorough, knowledge-transferring outcomes of the vulnerability assessments. If you need to prioritize, I recommend you start with a series of ongoing vulnerability assessments and then later add a bug bounty program if it makes sense for you. I would advise against starting with the bug bounty program because it's likely that you'd slip into a false sense of confidence: as you see vulnerabilities submitted, you may start to feel like the program is making you more secure. It would be doing that to some extent (which is great!). However, you might lose sight of the limitations of bug bounty programs. By starting with vulnerability assessments, you get all of the benefits of dedicated, thorough testing, *and* you avoid that complacency trap.

This book is written to help you find vulnerabilities, fix them, and prove your app is secure. Vulnerability assessments are the best way to do that, and so this book focuses on the outcomes they deliver. This is the last we'll discuss bug bounty programs, but given that you'll almost certainly consider one of these programs at some point, now you have context for how they fit in.

START WITH THE GOAL

Every single day, we are asked if we can help someone with their need for "penetration testing." However, before we ever answer, we always ask a clarifying question: "What do you want to achieve?"

That's what really matters. If we know the goal, we can figure out how to help. Sometimes you do indeed need a penetration test. Other times you need something else.

If you have a mature, heavily hardened system that's already been through extensive security testing and you want to know how it stands up to a simulated attack against a specific area, get penetration testing.

If you need to find basic, common issues quickly, keep costs to a minimum, and are fine without finding custom exploits, get vulnerability scanning.

If you need to find as many security vulnerabilities as possible—including especially custom exploits—understand their severity, and fix them based on priority ranking, get vulnerability assessments.[14]

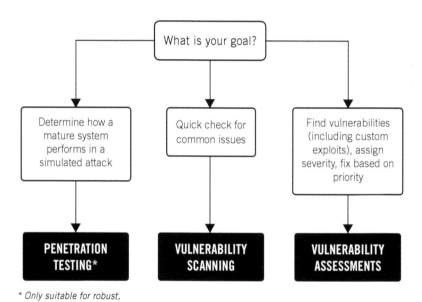

What is your goal?

Determine how a mature system performs in a simulated attack

Quick check for common issues

Find vulnerabilities (including custom exploits), assign severity, fix based on priority

PENETRATION TESTING*

VULNERABILITY SCANNING

VULNERABILITY ASSESSMENTS

* Only suitable for robust, thoroughly tested systems.

The point is this: each delivers different outcomes. Given that there is a specific outcome you're seeking, it's important

---

14 For further reading on the distinction between these concepts, take a look at the excellent blog by security researcher Daniel Miessler. Here's a good article to start with: Daniel Miessler, "The Difference between a Vulnerability Assessment and a Penetration Test," *DavidMiessler.com*, December 17, 2019, https://danielmiessler.com/study/vulnerability-assessment-penetration-test/.

that you do three things. First, understand there is a difference between these terms. Second, be super clear on your goal. Third, get the type of testing that delivers the outcome you're looking for (while ensuring you understand what your partner will actually deliver, irrespective of what term they use).

If you're like most software companies, your goal is probably to achieve a comprehensive understanding of your application's security so you can improve it. Then you want to prove it to your customers. Vulnerability assessments are the best way to achieve those outcomes, which is why this book skews toward that approach.

Some providers will fit neatly into one of these categories; others may deliver outcomes across domains (for example, we perform vulnerability assessments with a pen testing process for identifying exploitable vulnerabilities. Then we come back to test the remediations you implemented—a process I'll teach you about in chapter 5).

When you find yourself confused—which undoubtedly will happen—bring it back to your goal. Make it clear what you want to achieve, and push your security provider to clarify how the service achieves that goal. Don't relent until you understand. Don't decide based solely on the term they use, assuming what you *think* the provider means by it.

You now understand the different terms, but service providers will still confuse them. Like saying "cat" when they mean "horse," your customers and regulatory bodies will still say "penetration test" when they mean "vulnerability assessment." That isn't changing anytime soon. However, now that you are armed with these insights, you can guide everyone to the outcomes you need.

*The one you
(most likely) want*

	PENETRATION TESTING	VULNERABILITY SCANNING	VULNERABILITY ASSESSMENTS
IS KINDA LIKE	A single type of car crash test	Diagnostic scanner for "check engine" light	Safety engineering
IS SUITABLE FOR	Only mature, thoroughly tested systems	All levels of maturity	All levels of maturity
DELIVERS	Can a specific exploit outcome be achieved: Yes or No	Common, known vulnerabilities	Vulnerabilities (including custom exploits), severity ratings, how to fix

BIG IDEAS

Security terms are not interchangeable. If you use the wrong term, you'll get the wrong thing. Make sure you get the right thing.

- You're asking for penetration testing, but being sold vulnerability scanning. Yet, what you (probably) need are vulnerability assessments.

- Penetration testing is a time-constrained effort to verify whether or not a singular outcome is possible; it's only suitable for mature, hardened systems.

- Vulnerability scanning is a low-cost, low-effort exercise to quickly find basic issues. It includes false positives and inappropriate severity ratings.

- Vulnerability assessments are thorough, manual efforts to identify and prioritize security vulnerabilities. The objective is to find as many as possible and remediate them. As a result, you understand and reduce risk.

- Bug bounty programs are formalized crowdsourcing initiatives that reward security researchers for finding flaws in a company's technology.

- You can do vulnerability assessments alone, or you can combine vulnerability assessments with a bug bounty program. But you shouldn't do a bug bounty program alone.

- Be clear on your goal to make sure you get the outcomes you need, irrespective of which term is being used to refer to the testing.

For downloadable templates, team exercises, and real-world examples, go to *tedharrington.com/hackable*.

Once you know what type of testing you need, the next question is: what does it actually entail? Start with the fundamentals, then abuse functionality, chain exploits, and hunt for the unknown unknowns.

CHAPTER 4

HACK YOUR SYSTEM

LIE
We do security testing already.

TRUTH
We must go deeper.

Y ou can't demolish a building with just a chain.

Without a wrecking ball attached to it, you'd just be slapping a chain against a wall. Not much demolition will result. As discussed, when your security approach relies on scanners alone, that's all you're doing. Here's a better way:

"Think bad thoughts and ask hard questions."

One of our security analysts taught me that. By "bad thoughts," he means that you need to think like an attacker. By "hard questions," he means that you need to identify the assumptions made by the developer and then undermine those assumptions.

"Where the two meet," he told me, "is where you find security vulnerabilities that matter."

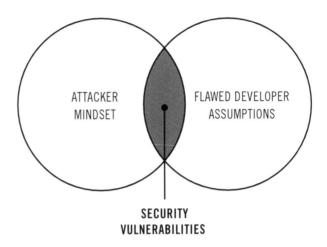

ATTACKER MINDSET

FLAWED DEVELOPER ASSUMPTIONS

**SECURITY
VULNERABILITIES**

Too many companies approach security without either. *You must do both.* Here's how.

Break your system. First, get the fundamentals: analyze the design, run scanners, and look for known vulnerabilities. Second, get the advanced tactics: abuse functionality, chain exploits, and seek the unknowns.

WHO DOES THE HACKING?

All of the methods in this chapter are executed by your external security partner. This is pretty standard practice, but for the sake of clarity, let me explain why.

You want an unbiased, objective view. They didn't build your code, so they have no attachment to it. You want to capitalize on subject matter expertise that you probably don't have in-house (or even if you do have ethical hackers in-house—which few companies do—you can augment those capabilities with the breadth and depth of an external, multidimensional team). You want someone to expose your blind spots, which, by definition, you are blind to. You want someone to find flaws and help you get better. Your customers can trust your security claims because it's an objective, unbiased authority stating *facts*, as opposed to you stating *opinions*.

All that said, nothing prevents your in-house personnel from doing as many of these elements as they're capable of, too. In fact, if they can, they should! More security is better than less security. Always. Just note that any testing done by in-house teams would be in *addition* to the testing done by your external partner. In-house personnel wouldn't be replacing the need for an external partner nor even reducing the scope of what your partner does (because that would make them less effective, and it would undermine the independence they deliver. You're going to need that independence later in the sales process, which we'll discuss in chapter 10). The real value in this method is going to come from external experts.

Whether you leave this entirely to external experts or augment it with your own people, it's crucial that you address this simple, harsh truth: most security testing falls woefully short of what is outlined in these pages.

Woefully short.

If you have valuable assets to protect, you want to make absolutely sure that you're getting all of these techniques from your security partner. If you are not, find out why. If they can't do these things, find a new partner. If they can do these things but they're not, find out why. It's probably due to either some miscommunication between you both or because you cut the budget so far that they are too constrained to do the stuff that matters (in chapter 7, we'll explore how to determine an appropriate budget). Either way, you *must* understand what you're getting. If you have assets worth protecting, your testing absolutely needs to entail all of what you're about to learn.

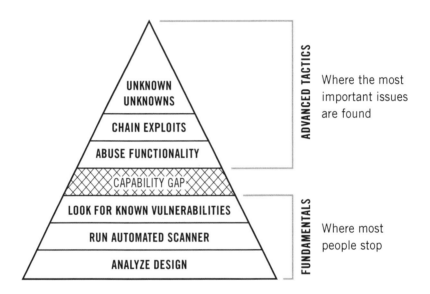

ANALYZE DESIGN

To understand how to break the system, your partner first needs to understand how it's supposed to work. They should learn the fundamentals of the app: the features, how users navigate through it, how access is provisioned, and where users can input values. They need to understand why it exists, what business problems it solves, and what it protects. Even two systems with similar features have remarkably different attack scenarios based on their use case. For example, an application used in the creation of movies has different attack conditions to consider than a similar application used in financial services. However—and quite disconcertingly—many security-testing services don't care how the app works. The

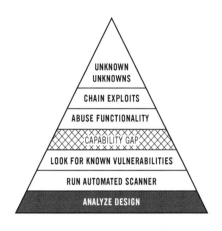

cheap, commodity scans that flood your Google searches all skip this step. It doesn't matter to a scanner what the system is used for or how it works. But to do the important steps that come later, you can't skip this one. Your partner needs to know how the app works so they can figure out how to abuse it. This is why we hire so many computer scientists, because they know how to build things, which helps them understand where the things might be broken.

Another crucial element of this stage is evaluating for design flaws, which are vulnerabilities inherent in the way you designed the system. A design vulnerability is when the system works *exactly* how it's supposed to and yet enables an attacker to exploit the system anyway (we'll explore the difference between design flaws and implementation flaws in chapter 5).

RUN AUTOMATED SCANNER

Scans are efficient and inexpensive and provide you with information that helps in later assessment stages. They quickly reveal the obvious issues that would require enormous effort to do manually. Most attackers run scans first, so it's a good idea

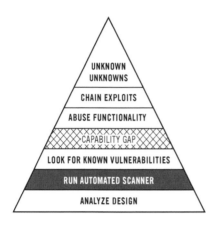

for you to do this, too. You want to see what they'll see. Just remember that scanning is *not* a comprehensive effort to find your security vulnerabilities. It's just one piece of the overall puzzle.

LOOK FOR KNOWN VULNERABILITIES

Many apps suffer the same mistakes. Yours probably does, too. Your attackers know this. They're just like you and me; they want the best results for the effort they invest, so the logical place to start is by looking where most people make mistakes. They seek these out as a shortcut to their success. To defend successfully, your testing must check for common issues. Examples include Cross-Site Scripting (XSS), which enables attackers to inject malicious scripts into web pages viewed by other users;

Cross-Site Request Forgery (CSRF), where a third-party web page can trick a user's browser into sending unauthorized commands to a web application; Broken Authentication, which is a failure to verify user identity; and Broken Access Control, which is a failure to enforce user permissions. This is just a sampling of the ever-evolving types of issues your attackers know to look for. Your security partner should, too. Some of these issues can be found with scanners, and some can only be found with manual assessment. Your in-house team might be able to do some of this. Your external partner definitely needs to do this.

The combination of these first three ideas makes up the fundamentals of your security-testing program. All of it is performed by your security partner, some of which your in-house team can help with, too.

However, you're not done yet. The valuable part is about to begin.

THERE'S A CAPABILITY GAP

Unfortunately, most security testing calls it quits at this point. Many approaches don't even hit everything we've discussed so far: they rely solely on scans and fail to analyze the design.

However, the majority of the value of security testing lies in what comes next. You don't want to leave it out.

There's a dramatic capabilities gap that separates the fundamentals from the advanced tactics. The testing we've discussed so far requires minimal to moderate skill and experience and can be performed with heavy emphasis on automated tools. But what comes

next—the stuff that *really* matters—requires high skill, deep experience, and a manual emphasis. It's incredibly difficult to do the things on the other side of this gap. You can't automate them; there's no tool for it. You need someone with the kind of deep expertise in manual assessment that you already learned is in short supply.

To achieve your security mission, you *must* live on the other side of that capabilities gap. Reject the hype: you can't do that with tools alone. It takes time, effort, and money to do things manually with deep subject matter expertise—but it's the *only way* to find your most critical security vulnerabilities.

Let's jump across the capability gap now.

ABUSE FUNCTIONALITY

Hacking is making something behave differently than it was intended to. A powerful technique to do that is by abusing functionality, which uses an application's own features in an attack.

A friend once told me this story about his high school's vending machine. Like most kids, he wanted to buy a lot of candy but didn't have a lot of money. This vending machine worked like any other vending machine: you put bills into a slot, the machine verifies the denomination, and it lets you select a treat. Here's the crucial detail: the intended functionality was to *ingest* bills, but there was no mechanism to prevent him from pulling the bills back out. All he needed to do was figure out how to do that. So here's what he did: he attached a piece of dental floss to a dollar bill. He'd insert the bill into the receptor, the vending machine would register payment is received, and he'd pick his treat. Then he would pull the bill back out with the dental floss. Over and over again. Nothing prevented him from doing this. Without even needing to talk to a single person who built that vending machine, I can tell you that *the system wasn't supposed to work that way.*

Nevertheless, it did.

That's a great example of abusing functionality.

Bad assumptions are commonly made about what users will (or won't) do. Over the years, I've heard some head-scratchers such as, "Oh, the user will never do it that way," or "This will always be safe," and my all-time favorite, "No one would think of *that*" (which is hilarious, because it's said in response to us *literally* thinking of exactly "*that*" and asking about it). These are absurd. Yet people say them. *All. The. Time.* The reason for this is a simple and human one: most people don't think like attackers. They see the good in the world and how things are supposed to be, not the bad in the world and how to break things. If that sounds like you, too, that's OK! That's why this book exists and why you work with external security experts who *do* think those bad thoughts every day. Nevertheless, assumptions about user behavior are the core of your security model. Bad assumptions severely weaken it. To be secure, you *must* identify those assumptions. You must understand how they'll be undermined. Abusing functionality is about asking "What if?" in order to turn assumptions upside down. Some examples of good "what-if" questions include:

- The username field is expecting up to twenty characters; what if I input two thousand?

- The input field is expecting alphanumeric characters; what if I input a command?

- The web app is forcing me to log in; what if I manually point the URL to a different page in the web app?

- The input field is expecting data; what if I input no data and click the button anyway?

Consider Manfred, a very successful online game hacker. One of his techniques was to exploit errors in how software handles numbers. This enabled him to obtain nearly unlimited in-game currency and then sell it to other gamers—for *real* money. The technique worked because the developers didn't expect gamers to use the system the way Manfred did.

Here's how it worked.

Most online games have in-game currency for buying things like weapons and skills upgrades. Games have "banks" to facilitate transactions, which are essentially computed like this:

$$(current\ account\ balance) - (withdrawal\ sum) = \\ (new\ account\ balance)$$

For example, if you have 500 coins and wanted to withdraw 100 of them, it would look like this:

$$(500\ coins) - (100\ coins) = (400\ coins)$$

Manfred exploited a vulnerability that enabled him to use *negative* integers instead of *positive* integers. So instead of withdrawing 100 coins, he would withdraw –100 coins. As you learned in middle school, subtracting a negative number is actually addition! As a result, this would happen:

$$(500 \; coins) - (-100 \; coins) = (600 \; coins)$$

Manfred would *increase* his account balance and get the withdrawn funds. He estimated the market value of his accumulated coins to be worth $397 trillion USD. That's of course a hilarious sum that is throttled by the actual market demand, but the point is this: the system was not supposed to do that. The developers didn't expect users to do this (and they certainly didn't want it to work this way). Manfred undermined that assumption. As he said in a profile about his work: "The best hacks are the invisible ones. You change the rules without anyone knowing what's going on."[15]

Interestingly, it turns out that the companies who made it hardest to tamper with the game were usually the ones with the most egregious security vulnerabilities. They incorrectly assumed that hackers would give up if it was hard to tamper with the game. As a result, they failed to invest in proper security testing. They didn't anticipate that a dedicated game hacker would put in the effort to defeat the anti-tampering mechanisms and abuse functionality.

---

15 Lorenzo Franceschi-Bicchiera, "For 20 Years, This Man Has Survived Entirely by Hacking Online Games," *Motherboard*, July 29, 2020, https://www.vice.com/en_us/article/59p7qd/this-man-has-survived-by-hacking-mmo-online-games.

That's why you need to do it as part of your security testing, because your attackers definitely will. You can't automate it. There's no tool that can do this for you. You need to do it manually.

CHAIN EXPLOITS

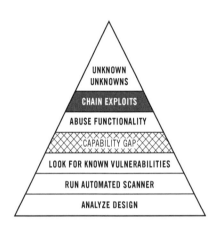

Exploit chaining is combining two or more vulnerabilities in order to multiply impact.

When I was a kid, one of my neighbors had a trampoline. One day, we discovered the "double jump." If one kid lands just as another kid jumps, it launches that second kid much higher than he could jump alone. I was propelled so high that I hit the tree branches towering overhead. I experienced a moment of weightlessness and then came crashing back down to earth. It was terrifying! But it was also enlightening: that day, I learned that two actions become exponentially more powerful when paired together. I can jump only so high, and my friend can jump only so high, but when they're combined into the "double jump," I get launched *scared-to-death* high.

That's what chaining exploits is like: combining things to magnify impact.

In a recent security assessment of an application that manages delivery of maintenance services (such as plumbing and electrical), we found a way to chain three vulnerabilities:

1. Sequential identifiers

2. Broken authorization

3. Cross-site scripting (XSS)

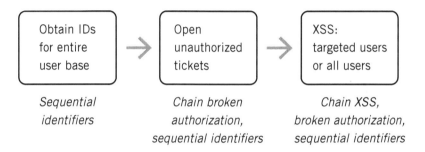

Obtain IDs for entire user base	Open unauthorized tickets	XSS: targeted users or all users
Sequential identifiers	*Chain broken authorization, sequential identifiers*	*Chain XSS, broken authorization, sequential identifiers*

- **Issue #1:** "Sequential identifiers" is a strategic weakness that makes it easy to predict sensitive account information: account IDs are numbered in order, rather than being randomized. For example, my account number is 0001, yours is 0002, your friend's is 0003, and so on. This means that an attacker can predict account IDs. Predictability makes it easier for an attacker to achieve widespread compromise across the entire user base of an application.

- **Issue #2:** Broken authorization is a vulnerability where an application fails to properly verify a user's permissions. In this case, the system didn't enforce authorization on the API used to open maintenance tickets. This means that an attacker can create maintenance tickets for any account, including those that the attacker is not a member of. Because the attacker can predict account IDs (as noted in issue #1), the attacker can do this to every user of the application.

- **Issue #3**: On the web page where maintenance tickets are viewed, the application failed to sanitize user input, a mechanism that prevents an attacker from entering malicious data. This means that when creating false tickets for victim accounts, if an attacker includes XSS payloads in those tickets, the system won't stop it. The attack payloads are delivered to unwitting victims.

Because an attacker can predict every account ID and create false tickets for them that include attack payloads, which the system fails to prevent, it means that *any* user of the application can be attacked successfully. The attacker can target a specific company or target every company. It means that simply by licensing an application, a user can be attacked by other users. It means that a user's confidential data—which the app is supposed to protect—might be accessed by other users of the app, including especially malicious users.

Nightmare scenarios like this are exactly what most enterprise buyers fear when licensing applications.

In isolation, each of these vulnerabilities is bad. In combination, they're catastrophic. Vulnerabilities must be considered in the context of each other, rather than in isolation. Attackers seek to chain exploits, and you should, too. There's no tool for this. You can't automate it. You must do it manually.

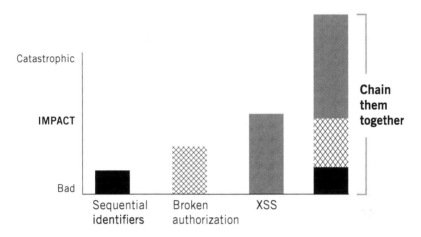

CHAINING EXPLOITS: GOING FROM BAD TO WORSE

UNKNOWN UNKNOWNS

In 1955, American psychologists developed the idea of "unknown unknowns."[16] It has entrenched itself in security vocabulary ever since. The idea is that there are three types of issues:

- **Known knowns**: flaws that you know about and that impact you. These are the vulnerabilities you've discovered through security assessments.

---

16 Communication Theory, "The Johari Window Model," September 30, 2020, https://www.communicationtheory.org/the-johari-window-model/.

- **Known unknowns**: flaws you know exist but may or may not affect you. These are the common classes of vulnerabilities that are persistently found in the world, such as XSS, CSRF, or broken authentication. You're not sure yet if they exist in your system. Also included in this group are widespread vulnerabilities that have a patch (a set of changes to a computer system that fixes a flaw in it), but you haven't implemented the patch (whether because you're unaware it exists or you just haven't gotten around to it. Both cases are extremely common).

- **Unknown unknowns**: flaws so unexpected you don't even consider them. This comes in numerous forms, including novel versions of common vulnerabilities, zero-days in the supply chain, and previously unknown attack methods.

A CTO once humorously said to me, "Ted, I don't like monsters. And I don't like getting bitten in the butt. But I don't even know what the monsters are, or when they'd jump up and bite me in the butt." This memory always brings a smile to my face, not just because it's ridiculous phrasing, but also because it's the best description I've ever heard of a common fear: "I don't know what I don't know." Even if you haven't admitted it out loud to anyone, I'm guessing you've felt that fear too at some point.

You resolve that concern by turning unknowns into knowns.

Dealing with unknown unknowns is the absolute pinnacle of security testing. It entails the most important issues you'll face. It's where your focus needs to be. Unfortunately, most security testing actually doesn't focus on these issues. Tool-based

Unknown Unknowns

Type	What It Is	What to Do about It
Novel Versions of Known Vulnerability Classes	Types of vulnerabilities that are known to persistently exist (such as XSS) but where instances of it are unique to you.	Tools and automation may help find some of these issues, but the emphasis is on manual investigation.
Zero-Days in the Supply Chain	When components that are out of your control have critical flaws in them (as was the case with Heartbleed, a vulnerability in the open source code library that implemented critical security protocols).	You likely can't or won't perform assessments on the supply chain, so your best approach is Defense in Depth (which you'll learn about in chapter 9).
Previously Unknown Attack Methods	New techniques that you haven't seen before (such as request smuggling, which we'll discuss in a moment).	Only discoverable with skilled manual investigation.

approaches all settle for the easily discoverable, known issues and go no further. Even most manual approaches lack the skill, experience, or sophistication to help you resolve unknown unknowns. To find the unknown unknowns requires skilled manual investigation. It is the *only* way to solve this part of the security puzzle.

To illustrate, consider request smuggling. It's an attack technique that abuses discrepancies in how different pieces of software process inputs. Web apps get lots of requests and need a way to handle them. There are two ways to do this: with one expensive server or multiple cheap servers. It's usually a better business decision to use multiple cheap servers. When you do that, you need load balancing, which is a process to distribute the requests. Imagine it like a traffic cop pointing some cars into the left lane and some cars into the right lane. As a result, this means you now have two types of software: the load balancing software and the server software. These are intended to process inputs the same way; however, sometimes their implementations differ slightly. For example, if a request is supposed to end in a specific format but it doesn't, each system independently determines what to do. When there's a mismatch in how the pieces of software handle those requests, attackers can smuggle in a malicious request alongside a legitimate one. The load balancer would submit both as a single, legitimate request, but the server would then execute it as two requests—one legitimate and one malicious. There are endless things an attacker could do with this, such as change permissions to admin rights or leak passwords of other users.

REQUEST SMUGGLING

This vulnerability is incredibly specific to your system's configuration and your application's logic. Attacking it requires a custom exploit. It wasn't even documented as an attack technique until *sixteen years* (!) after it became possible.[17] You simply cannot find complex yet catastrophic issues like this with a tool alone. Your investigation absolutely must be by a skilled human, solving problems manually.

As one CIO put it, "Security is all of the problems you don't know about yet." That's why this method matters. It helps you understand your problems so you can solve them. However, it only works if you go the whole way. Settling for half measures like tools alone is not going to cut it. In the last chapter, you learned about the distinction between security terms. What you need usually requires every element of this method that you just learned. However, when "penetration testing" is really just "vulnerability scanning," all you're getting are a few of the easier elements (running a scanner that looks for common, known vulnerabilities).

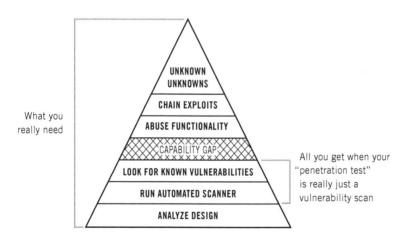

What you really need

UNKNOWN UNKNOWNS
CHAIN EXPLOITS
ABUSE FUNCTIONALITY
CAPABILITY GAP
LOOK FOR KNOWN VULNERABILITIES
RUN AUTOMATED SCANNER
ANALYZE DESIGN

All you get when your "penetration test" is really just a vulnerability scan

---

17 HTTP requests were first invested in 1991. The first documented discussion of request smuggling was in 2005. Even today, it's still not a commonly understood attack technique, and there's still no automated way to search for it.

Instead, make sure you're getting this method. Make sure you're getting all of it. When done right, this method goes far beyond those fundamental steps. This method ensures that your most important security vulnerabilities will likely be found so you can fix them and prove that your app is secure. This is how you build a better, more secure product that your customers are comfortable using.

DOES IT WORK, THOUGH?

Here's some data about outcomes this method delivers. It's drawn from fifty-one security assessments spanning 7,514 hours in which 720 vulnerabilities were discovered.

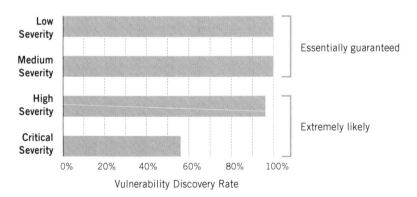

LIKELIHOOD OF DISCOVERING VULNERABILITIES USING THIS METHOD

The data shows that using this method, our analysts discovered *critical* vulnerabilities in 56 percent of assessments, plus *high* severity flaws in 96 percent of them. Medium and low severity issues are pretty much a guarantee, discovered 100 percent of the time.

This method works.

In chapter 5, we'll cover what severity ratings mean and what to do with them. But for now, the takeaway is a simple one. If your goal is to find vulnerabilities so you can fix them and prove your app is secure, *this is the way to do it.*

The power of this method lies on the other side of that capability gap. The most important outcomes are delivered when you abuse functionality, chain exploits, and seek the unknown unknowns. Compared to basic methods like scanning alone, this method is harder, takes longer, and costs more. But those investments pale in comparison to the impact you'll make on your security mission. This method brings the wrecking ball to the demolition. It helps you smash the system so you can get better.

BIG IDEAS

Break your system. First, get the fundamentals: analyze the design, run scanners, and look for known vulnerabilities. Second, get the advanced tactics: abuse functionality, chain exploits, and seek the unknowns.

- The security-testing method outlined in this chapter is performed by your external partner (though there are elements that in-house resources could do in addition). If you have valuable assets to protect, you want to make *absolutely* sure that you're getting all of these techniques from your security partner.

- First, get the fundamentals.
  - Analyze the design. To understand how to break the system, your partner first needs to understand how it's supposed to work.
  - Run scans. These quickly reveal the obvious issues that would require enormous effort to do manually.
  - Look for known vulnerabilities. Many apps suffer the same mistakes. Yours probably does, too. To defend successfully, your testing must check for common issues.

- There's a dramatic capabilities gap that separates the fundamentals from the stuff that matters, which requires high skill, deep experience, and a manual emphasis.

- Second, get the advanced tactics.
  - Abuse functionality in order to use an application's own features in an attack.
  - Chain exploits by combining two or more vulnerabilities in order to multiply impact. Vulnerabilities must be considered in the context of each other, rather than in isolation.
  - Seek the unknown unknowns, the flaws so unexpected you don't even consider them. This is the pinnacle of security testing.

For downloadable templates, team exercises, and real-world examples, go to *tedharrington.com/hackable*.

Now that you know how to find the most important vulnerabilities, you need to fix them.

CHAPTER 5

FIX YOUR VULNERABILITIES

LIE

Remediations are painful, expensive, and take a long time.

TRUTH

With the right approach, remediations are easily managed.

When it comes to making mistakes, school got it wrong. School taught us that making mistakes is bad. Teachers literally punished us for making mistakes on homework, quizzes, and tests.

But that's not the real world. Mistakes happen, and that's OK. The very nature of software development is that mistakes will be made and vulnerabilities will be introduced. Again, that's OK— *as long as you do something about it.*

What's *not* OK is failing to fix mistakes. What's *not* OK is failing to learn from mistakes. What's *not* OK is continuing to make the same mistakes over and over.

A security consultant's job is not done until the client gets better. For that reason, I'm fond of having meetings at the conclusion of security assessments to review the reports and ensure that our customers understand the issues. I want them to take action.

It was after one such project that I found myself in a massive boardroom. It was filled with the executives responsible for the security of a whole portfolio of applications. They sat patiently as we described vulnerability after vulnerability and how an attacker would exploit each. There were hundreds of them.

This moment was the fork in the road: the companies who achieve security excellence use their vulnerabilities to drive their success. Those who won't, don't. This sometimes happens when people get discouraged by seeing how much work remediations require. As a result, they simply postpone them—*indefinitely*. To be fair, they don't intentionally postpone indefinitely, but that's what winds up happening. It's easier that way, sure, but it also guarantees you won't ever achieve security excellence.

As I stood in that boardroom, I was dying to know which group this company would fall into. Would they fix or forget?

We finished describing the last exploit sequence and then shut up. Moments passed. No one said anything. The silence hung heavily in the room.

Then a chair squeaked.

The VP sponsoring the project leaned back in his chair. He gestured to the screen that was still showing an exploit sequence and looked around the table at his peers. The look on his face clearly meant, *"This is what I've been saying!"*

He was in.

I'll never forget that moment. It's what security consultants live for: when you know you'll be able to help your client get better because they're *ready* to get better.

So are *you* ready to get better? Now that your vulnerabilities have been found, it's time to put in the work to get the results you desire.

Fixing your vulnerabilities is a three-phase process: prioritize, remediate, and verify.

REMEDIATIONS

Remediations fix your vulnerabilities. They come either as resolutions (which completely fix the flaw) or as mitigations (which minimize exploitability or reduce severity). Either way, there are three things you'll want to do:

1. Prioritize vulnerabilities by severity

2. Remediate your vulnerabilities

3. Verify the remediations

HOW TO FIX SECURITY VULNERABILITIES

Once you've done each of these steps, you get a better, more secure system. You also get a sales benefit, too: you can prove it.

While your competitors struggle to deliver the security that your customers demand, you now have a competitive advantage. In chapter 10, I'll give you prescriptive, step-by-step guidance on exactly how to prove the security of your application. However, before you can do that, you need to fix your vulnerabilities first.

Here's how.

STEP 1: PRIORITIZE VULNERABILITIES BY SEVERITY RATING

Once you've found your issues, you need to understand how severe they are. Vulnerabilities are not all the same; some are catastrophic, whereas others are not. Severity is a combination of exposure and impact.

EXPOSURE + IMPACT = SEVERITY

- How accessible a vulnerable system is
- How easily an attack can be performed

- How valuable an asset is
- How much damage results if an asset is compromised

- How significant the issue is
- How you should prioritize remediation efforts

Vulnerability severity balances many factors, including attacker skill, motivation, access, and resources. It accounts for the complexity of both the system and the attack. It considers how easy the vulnerability would be to exploit and how catastrophic the outcome would be if that happened. It helps you figure out what to remediate first.

This phase of the effort is done collaboratively between your in-house teams and your security partner. Usually, what happens is your security partner assigns the severity rating, and you work with them to adjust if needed. For example, if there's a mitigating factor in your business that you forgot to mention, which would alter how severe an issue is, this is when that might come up.

Grading severity is an imperfect science. It's highly dependent on your specific situation, and security professionals may vary slightly in how they define or measure it. No matter what, though, severity ratings should be customized to the system evaluated. (However, note that automated tools usually don't customize severity ratings at all.)

Irrespective of how severity is determined, vulnerabilities typically fall into categories: critical, high, medium, and low (we also use a category for informational issues).

Critical	Readily exploitable or substantially exposed and would deliver excessive damage.
High	Heavily expose the system but demand additional attack requirements.
Medium	Not a significant risk to the system alone but could lead to exploitation if combined with other issues.
Low	Partial exposure but not an immediate threat to the most valuable assets.
Info	Unlikely to threaten the system currently but could become an issue if future changes to the system alter exposure or impact.

Use severity ratings to prioritize your remediation efforts. For example:

- **Critical and High:** stop everything and address these issues right now.

- **Medium, Low, and Info:** integrate remediations into your development roadmap, addressing these issues as quickly as you can.

Fix the most dangerous vulnerabilities first, then plan how to address the rest. That's how you manage the security workload into your other development priorities.

STEP 2: REMEDIATE YOUR VULNERABILITIES

Next, you need to actually fix the vulnerabilities. If you don't, you waste the time, money, and effort you invested in finding them. This phase of effort is usually done in-house by your developers. (In reality, you *could* have your security partner do this if they have software development capabilities, but you'd be paying consulting rates to do work that you already have in-house capabilities for. So it doesn't usually make sense to outsource this part, unless your business model already includes outsourcing development, too.)

You'd be surprised how often people skip this and literally don't fix their vulnerabilities. It may be hard, take time, and divert attention, but it needs to be done. Otherwise, what was the point?

We recently finished the first project for a new customer. A couple of weeks after submitting the report to them, we still hadn't heard back, despite our best efforts to follow up. We didn't know whether they'd read or even received the report, or how remediations were going. This was mildly alarming because their report was absolutely *packed* with dangerous vulnerabilities we'd found in their system. It included insecure input handling, unvalidated HTTPS certificates, and globally accessible secrets.[18] One particularly nasty example was that it had a remote code execution (RCE) vulnerability, a security flaw that enables an attacker to execute commands or code, thereby controlling how the system behaves.

Eventually, we got the CTO on the phone. Through probing questions, we discovered what was going on: the CTO was daunted by the amount of work the remediations were going to require. He didn't want to tack that effort on top of everything else that his developers had to do. He didn't want to see deadlines slip. He didn't want them to redo work they'd already done. He was a little embarrassed to have seen his team introduce so many vulnerabilities. So he simply decided to ignore the report.

That's a bummer for everybody. It's a bummer for the developers, who missed the chance to get better. It's a bummer for the CTO, who made important business decisions with flawed reasoning. It's a bummer for us to fail to help them, especially since they needed it.

The story has a sad ending: a few months later, they suffered one of the biggest security breaches in their industry's history. It was disheartening for everyone.

---

18 Don't worry about what each of these mean; just know that these are very bad.

I'm telling this story because you need to recognize that done right, a security assessment is going to result in some work to do. That's OK! It's good for you! Expect this; don't avoid it. You'll be better as a result.

As far as *how* to do the remediations, that advice is pretty straightforward: follow the guidance outlined in your security assessment report! Assuming you got the right partner and the right kind of testing, this part is as simple as it gets. The instructions are literally right there for you in the report deliverable, and your security partner can guide you if you get confused. You've already prioritized the vulnerabilities by severity; now you just need to work through remediating them.

STEP 3: VERIFY THE REMEDIATIONS

Once you've fixed your issues, you need to ensure the remediations work. This is an effort known as remediation testing (or sometimes casually referred to as mitigation testing). This phase of effort is performed by your security partner, who checks the work your developers did to fix the issues.

Remediation testing confirms a few things:

1. **The remediations are done right.** Sometimes there are miscommunications or misunderstandings, resulting in remediations being done wrong. That's OK—as long as you check for it. Remediation testing is your safety net to make sure that you get them right.

2. **The remediations work.** Sometimes the remediation doesn't fully solve the problem. Sometimes it leaves

room for a more nuanced, expanded attack scenario that is still viable even with the remediation implemented. Remediation testing catches these issues.

3. **The remediations do not introduce new vulnerabilities.** Anytime you make a change, you might accidentally introduce a new weakness. Remediation testing checks for that, too.

Remediation testing delivers the ultimate payoff for all your hard work: an updated report that shows vulnerabilities as resolved. This is valuable because it confirms—in writing—which issues are fixed. That gives you a super-powerful tool for your sales process because it shows your customers two things. First, that you go deep enough to find important vulnerabilities. Second, that you fix them. They'll absolutely love this. In chapter 10, I'll explain how to use your reports—including details on resolved vulnerabilities—to help you earn trust and win sales.

VULNERABILITIES: DESIGN VS. IMPLEMENTATION

As you think about fixing your vulnerabilities, it's important to understand their nature. Where they came from impacts what you need to do to fix them.

Your vulnerabilities result either from how you designed the system or from how you implemented that design.

Implementation flaws are when the system works differently than intended. For example, you designed an authentication model that allows access for some users and prevents access for everyone else. A vulnerability like XSS enables an attacker to bypass that protection. You obviously didn't mean it to work that way, but nevertheless, it did. Issues like this happen when the design is fine, but you just made a mistake in how you executed it. Fixing these issues means correcting those mistakes.

By contrast, design flaws are issues with the design itself. They happen when the system works exactly as intended, and yet the attacker can use that intended functionality to exploit the system anyway. For example, you might implement rate limiting to lock an account that receives too many failed login attempts. However, if poorly designed, it could provide an attacker a way to intentionally trigger it across all users, making the system unusable. Fixing design-level issues requires you to adjust the design itself. Depending on the issue, that could be a tremendous undertaking (and is why you want to build security into the development process, which you'll learn about in chapter 9).

CASE STUDY: REMEDIATION TESTING

Let's tie it all together with a story.

In the course of a vulnerability assessment, we found that one of our customers' applications had a listening service that was open to the internet. This is bad. Even attackers without login credentials could access it. This meant that literally *anyone*, from anywhere in the world, could issue a command to the application's server. In particular, the system would respond to a command to delete files. This app hosts enormously valuable intellectual property; maliciously deleting any of it would be catastrophic.

This vulnerability needed to be fixed immediately. We recommended a remediation, and the customer implemented it quickly.

Shortly thereafter, we performed remediation testing. We confirmed that the remediation was effective against the dire attack scenario: an uncredentialed user could no longer attack from anywhere. That was good! However, we also discovered that a more nuanced attack was still possible. If successfully exploited, this would also result in file deletion.

The requirements of this more difficult attack were very high: the attacker needed to (a) control a domain name system (DNS) infrastructure (a distributed database system that resolves IP addresses, which are the unique identifiers for devices on a network), (b) control a domain name, (c) get a victim to visit a web page controlled by the attacker, and (d) keep the victim there for at least a minute while the attack runs. That's a high barrier, and so the likelihood of exploitation is much lower than the original issue. However, the impact remains the same: if successful, the attacker delivers the catastrophic compromise of file deletion.

Thanks to remediation testing, this issue was quickly resolved, too.

Therein lies the value of remediation testing. The original vulnerability was readily exploitable by anyone on the internet, existed in a production system actively being used, and exposed enormously valuable assets. Resolving it was exceptionally urgent. The remediation was developed and implemented quickly. It completely resolved the known attack scenario. With that remediation in place, we had time to further expand the attack scenario. We consulted security analysts on other teams, studied new approaches, and applied new techniques. As a result, we came back to remediation testing with new exploit techniques. The customer remediated those, too.

That's why remediation testing is so powerful. You fix your vulnerabilities, ranked by priority. You ensure that the fixes work. You expand attack scenarios.

Remediations matter. That's about as succinct as it gets. Do them and you'll get better; don't and you won't.

Achieving security excellence requires that you find and fix vulnerabilities. Be like that executive leaning back in his squeaky chair, signaling that it's time to get to work.

BIG IDEAS

Fixing your vulnerabilities is a three-phase process: prioritize, remediate, and verify.

- Remediations fix your vulnerabilities. They come either as resolutions (which completely fix the flaw) or as mitigations (which minimize exploitability or reduce severity).

- Prioritize vulnerabilities by severity. Address critical and high-severity issues immediately, and work everything else into your development roadmap.

- Remediate your vulnerabilities. You'd be surprised how often this gets skipped; if you do, you waste the time, money, and effort invested in finding the vulnerabilities in the first place.

- Verify the remediations. Remediation testing is the process by which you verify that the remediations you implemented are done right, solve the problem, and do not introduce new vulnerabilities.

- Implementation flaws are when the system works differently than intended. Design flaws are when the system works exactly as intended, but the attacker uses functionality to exploit the system anyway. How you fix the vulnerability depends on which type of flaw it is.

For downloadable templates, team exercises, and real-world examples, go to *tedharrington.com/hackable*.

Now that you know how to fix your vulnerabilities, you're done, right? No. Now you need to break your system again.

CHAPTER 6

HACK IT AGAIN

LIE
Once I'm done, I'm good.

TRUTH
If I'm good, I'm never done.

n karate, earning a black belt isn't the end of your journey; it's just the beginning. It's the same idea with application security: be proud of the work you've put in to get to this point, but you aren't finished. Things change, forcing you to adapt, which causes your security posture to change, too. Reassessments are how you deal with that reality.

Do reassessments right so they're more effective, less expensive, and deliver a better partnership.

SECURITY IS A LOOP, NOT A LINE

"Once you know the rules, the game changes." That's how a director of application security described how fast the world changes.

Change comes in many forms. All of them require you to revisit your security.

You develop your system constantly. If you're like most companies in the software business, you're relentlessly developing new features, streamlining workflows, and improving the user experience. Every single change to your platform changes your attack surface (which we'll talk more about in chapter 8). Whenever you update your application, you might introduce or alter threat vectors; you need to evaluate them for vulnerabilities.

Your development priorities shift. Maybe you see an opportunity in the market or learn that your customers want something that is currently backlogged on your development roadmap. As you adjust, your security model changes. You need to reevaluate how these changes impact your security. As you develop new code, you'll almost certainly inject new vulnerabilities. You need to address those, too.

Customer demands change. Sometimes they require new security controls. Sometimes they want to change their model, such as moving from software that is hosted on-premises (which runs at their physical site on computers they own and control) to software that is cloud-hosted (which runs remotely on computers owned and controlled by a service provider). Whatever the change, they need assurance that your security meets their new needs.

New attack techniques are invented. Attackers are constantly inventing new ways to exploit systems. You need to constantly investigate these new techniques, too. Security truly is an arms race, and you need to keep up.

Widespread vulnerabilities in core technologies are discovered. The very nature of building software is that you'll have dependencies. Whether that's on a cloud provider, third-party libraries, integration of third-party solutions, or some other shared component, your security relies on someone else's security to some extent. Those third parties are evolving, too, while at the same time, new exploits are discovered in them. You need to reevaluate your system to defend accordingly.

The point is this: change happens. Change impacts your security. To deal with that, you need to adapt. You want to be like the ultimate hackers: squirrels.

Yup, squirrels.

If you've ever seen a bird feeder, you've seen squirrels defeat almost any attempt to prevent them from stealing the feed. Squirrels don't care that the feed isn't for them. To the squirrel, it's about *survival*. Steal the feed or die. So they relentlessly adapt to whatever barrier is thrown at them.

That's the level of intensity you're up against. That's how your attackers think, and that's how you must, too.

Finally, most companies are unable to invest enough time or money to assess the *entire* solution at once. The way to handle this is by breaking it into components and rolling through them over time in subsequent reassessments. For example, you might first look at a web application's front end (the portion of an application that users interact with) and then later look at the back end (the servers, databases, and other portions of an application that enable the user-facing front end).

Many people mistake security as being a *linear* process. Do step A, then step B, then step C, and you're done. But that's wrong. Security is not a *line*; security is a *loop*. Yes, there is a process, but once you finish, you must *repeat* it. Forever. As an SVP of product management put it, "There's no finish line for security."

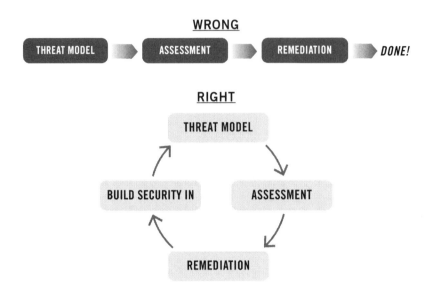

The process follows a simple formula:

1. **Establish/update your threat model** (we'll cover this in chapter 8).

2. **Perform security assessment** (as you learned in chapter 4).

3. **Remediate your vulnerabilities** (as you learned in chapter 5).

4. **Continue developing but with security in mind** (we'll cover this in chapter 9).

5. **Repeat** (as we'll discuss in this chapter).

Your security partner has found your vulnerabilities through security assessment; now they need to perform reassessments. In a reassessment, all of the same steps as the initial assessment happen. Analyze changes to the design. Run scans. Look for common vulnerabilities. Abuse functionality. Chain exploits. Look for unknown unknowns. You deploy the same methodology, mindset, and testing types. You pursue the same outcomes.

The initial assessment is *to break*. The reassessment is *to break again*.

THE IMPACT OF REASSESSMENTS

What additional value do reassessments deliver?

Short answer: a lot.

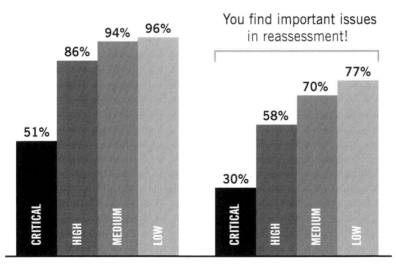

REASSESSMENTS: RATE OF FINDING VULNERABILITIES

Our data (as first introduced in chapter 4) shows that the impact is clear: important vulnerabilities continue to appear, even in later rounds of assessment. Critical vulnerabilities are found in 30 percent of reassessments, whereas high-severity vulnerabilities are found at nearly double that rate (58 percent of reassessments). A moment ago, we discussed how change impacts your security posture. These numbers quantify that impact. This data also powerfully supports the things you want to do:

- **Prove ROI**: Your chances are very high of finding the vulnerabilities that matter. This justifies your investment of time, money, and effort. After all, the point of security testing is to find issues (so you can fix them and then prove your security to your customers). The data demonstrates you will do exactly that.

- **Understand risk**: Because you know that issues will continue to appear, and you now have a statistical rate, you can quantify risk.

- **Reduce risk**: When you find the vulnerabilities that matter, you can eradicate them, which reduces risk.

Another way to consider the same data is *distribution* of vulnerabilities, which this graph shows. The data demonstrates that of all critical and high-severity vulnerabilities that are discovered, 7.78 percent of them are found in reassessments.

Pause to think about that. It means that for every one hundred vulnerabilities that exist, almost eight of them are critical

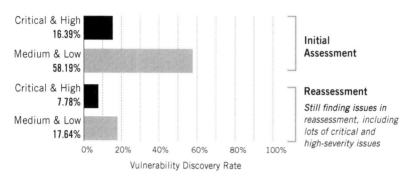

DISTRIBUTION OF VULNERABILITIES BY SEVERITY RATING:
INITIAL ASSESSMENT VS. REASSESSMENT

or high severity and will only be found in reassessment. No matter how many you find in the initial assessment, you will find more in reassessments.

For example, in recent reassessments, we've discovered critical vulnerabilities, such as unencrypted communications over cleartext HTTP, unauthenticated command injection in DNS testing script, command injection via admin interface, unauthenticated arbitrary file disclosure, API test methods exposed, unauthenticated command injection, unauthenticated XML external entity injection, insufficient authorization verification during login, insufficient authorization verification for adding users, and insufficient entropy for authentication challenge.[19] These issues were all the result of our clients developing code. Changes to code mean changes to the attack surface, which means new vulnerabilities may have been introduced. That's why reassessments matter. You want to catch those issues.

---

19 Again, for the sake of brevity, I'll spare the definitions on each of these. Simply understand that these are bad.

And those are just examples of the *critical* severity vulnerabilities! There are tons more that are high-severity, medium-severity, and low-severity vulnerabilities, too.

The point is this: eradicating issues like these is the point of security testing. You won't be free of them after just the initial assessment. Vulnerabilities continue to appear. Reassessments ensure you continue to identify them so you can fix them.

We have a client who is excellent at translating the results of security assessments into improved engineering practices. By their twelfth round of testing, we didn't find any security vulnerabilities at all. Same with the thirteenth and fourteenth rounds. However, on the fifteenth round, we found something major: a security vulnerability that would incur enormous GDPR fines.[20]

They had moved some of their document storage from on-premises to a cloud environment, failing to configure it properly in the process. As a result, anyone with internet access could navigate to their cloud storage, enumerate the file system, and obtain any files on that server. This customer deals in highly sensitive financial data, which these files contained. Every instance of unauthorized access would incur a fine. There were thousands of instances. The potential fine was well over $10,000,000.

Because the security assessment discovered the issue before attackers or regulators found it, they were able to eradicate it.

---

20 The General Data Protection Regulation 2016/679 (GDPR) is a regulation on data protection and privacy in the European Union (EU) and the European Economic Area (EEA). It also regulates the transfer of personal data outside the EU and EEA. Discussion of compliance programs is beyond the scope of this book, but the point here is simply that noncompliance results in hefty penalties.

Therein lies the value of reassessments: even though you'll introduce new vulnerabilities, you'll be able to catch them. If it happens even to a company like that one who has mature security practices, it happens to everyone. Reassessments address that reality. Reassessments are the lifeblood of your long-term security success.

THE RIGHT CADENCE FOR REASSESSMENTS

So how often should you have your security partner perform reassessments?

Short answer: frequently.

Probably more frequently than you currently are.

The right reassessment interval for most apps is every three to six months. Some require more or less frequency, but most fall into this range. However, many companies think about security only annually or every two years. Some consider it even less frequently than that.

The world changes rapidly. When you wait too long, you undermine your own security mission. Think back to a year ago, and consider what your technology looked like. Consider what your industry looked like. A lot has changed, right? And don't forget that your attackers have evolved, too. So why would it make sense to wait so long to reconsider security, with that much changing?

It doesn't.

If you hit the right cadence, you account for change. If you wait too long, you cede the advantage to your attackers. You leave yourself unnecessarily exposed for too long.

The time frame between assessments should be driven by a variety of factors, such as how rapidly you develop, how valuable your assets are, how much of an attack target you are, and how frequently your customers need assurance. As these factors increase, your time frame between assessments must decrease.

Unfortunately, many companies pace their reassessment intervals on some arbitrary time frame instead. This might be because compliance programs have latched on to the idea of "annual penetration testing" or because many enterprise buyers seem to suggest this, too. Many people think of security like an annual physical exam with your doctor: a necessary but annoying interruption that you do as infrequently as possible, and hope it doesn't bring bad news. Instead, think of it like nutrition: something you consider constantly. You shouldn't evaluate your sugar intake once a year; you should evaluate it regularly.

When you implement an appropriate assessment cadence rather than one that's too long, you'll find that it is more effective, less expensive, and delivers better partnership value.

BENEFIT #1:
THE RIGHT CADENCE IS MORE EFFECTIVE

When you perform assessments more frequently, you identify and remediate security vulnerabilities more quickly. You reduce opportunities for exploitation. You also accelerate knowledge transfer from your security experts to your developers. You get more opportunities to learn from mistakes. Your developers improve faster and introduce fewer vulnerabilities.

More frequent assessments deliver better security faster.

BENEFIT #2:
THE RIGHT CADENCE IS LESS EXPENSIVE

Security done at the right intervals is actually less expensive, too.

Yes, you read that right. This is one of those rare cases where the better path is also the better price.

When I was a little kid, my grandfather would hand me a few dollars at the end of every visit. "Some walking-around money," he'd call it. Even back then, I wanted to get the best bang for my buck; I can remember calculating how much candy I could buy. If you were just handed a few dollars, which would you rather do:

- buy six candies for $6 ($1/each)

- buy twelve candies for $5.40 ($0.45/each)

If we assume that whether you get six or twelve, it's the same quality candy, you'd want the latter right? You get more candy that costs less overall and costs less per piece.

Pretty cool, right?

That's what you get when you do reassessments at the appropriate intervals. You get more of the same deliciousness for a better price.

If that sounds too good to be true, let me explain the economics of security testing. It's pretty simple, really. Your initial assessment is always going to be the most involved effort and thus the most expensive. If you approach reassessments too infrequently, you're essentially getting an initial assessment every time. That means you pay for the more expensive version.

But if you hit the right intervals, you get a streamlined effort, which costs substantially less.

This is driven by two factors: learning curve and the ability to deal with change.

First, there's the learning curve—the effort required to ramp up to proficiency. Consider something you've mastered. Let's say a financial report that you present to the board. The first time that you prepare this report, you need to put in a lot of effort to figure it out. You need to learn about the audience, what they need to understand, and which questions need to be answered. Then you spend time collecting information, synthesizing data, preparing charts, creating slides, practicing the presentation, and delivering it. Later, after having done it several times, you're much quicker. You've cut out all the effort associated with the learning curve.

Second, there's the ability to deal with change. In pretty much anything anyone does, things change over time. That same financial report will eventually have to answer different questions for different people who care about different things and want to see information in different formats. When you're in a rhythm on the project, adapting to these changes is easier than if you didn't touch it for a long time.

Taken together, these factors deliver what is called *efficiency gain*. It's where you get faster the more you do something because you understand it better. It's when you're better able to adapt to changes because you're much more familiar. Once your security partner understands your business and your technology better, they become more efficient.

However, if you wait too long, you lose the efficiency gain. After six months, the benefits begin to dissipate. This is called the *efficiency cliff*: a steep decline in efficiency after too much time between activities.

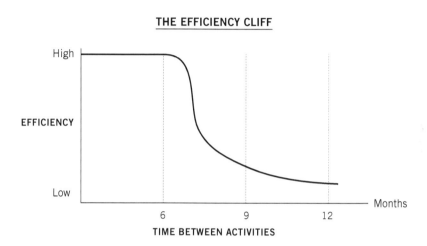

THE EFFICIENCY CLIFF

Imagine you didn't touch that financial report for a year. How efficient would you be when you picked it back up? Not very.

When reassessment cadence is too long, you need to duplicate the same investment in efficiency gain again. That is wasteful. If you are like most people in technology, you hate waste. You hate inefficiency. When you wait too long, you backslide on efficiency, thereby bringing your costs back up again. However, if you stay on the right cadence, you avoid that waste.

OK, so let's talk about how this makes things less expensive. Keep in mind that initial assessments require a learning curve and are less efficient in dealing with change, whereas reassessments do not require a learning curve and are more efficient in dealing with change (if you do them at appropriate intervals).

Most people mistakenly think of security assessments as an annual exercise, rather than something that needs to be done every three to six months (in most cases). Because annually is too long between assessments, that means that you wind up doing an initial assessment every time, which looks like this:

INEFFICIENT REASSESSMENT CADENCE

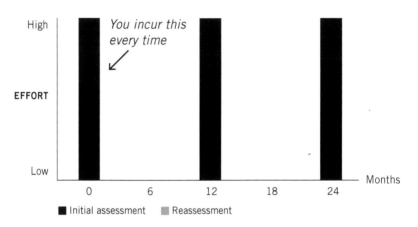

But when you use an appropriate cadence for reassessments, it means you only incur the initial assessment once, and then every reassessment after that costs way, way less. It looks like this:

APPROPRIATE REASSESSMENT CADENCE IS LESS EXPENSIVE

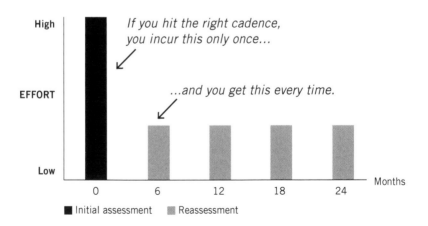

Think about how easy that is: just do it more regularly and you instantly slash your per-assessment cost.

A few years ago, we wanted to put hard numbers to this idea of efficiency gain, so our team analyzed ten years of data from our own security assessments. The result was startling: on average, a reassessment done at the proper cadence requires 60 percent less effort than the initial assessment of the same system. *Sixty percent less!*[21]

Let's model some numbers. Let's say an initial assessment costs $100,000.[22] A reassessment is 60 percent less, which would be $40,000. Let's imagine two companies: client A does annual security assessments, whereas client B does them at six-month intervals.

Comparing Per-Assessment Costs

	Client A	Client B
Cadence	12 months	6 months
Assessment 1	$100,000	$100,000
Assessment 2	$100,000	$40,000
Assessment 3	$100,000	$40,000
Assessment 4	$100,000	$40,000
Assessment 5	$100,000	$40,000
Assessment 6	$100,000	$40,000

---

21 I can't promise you that this data reflects what *every* security consultant might deliver for you, because I don't have access to everyone's data. But I can assure you that the method outlined in this book delivers these outcomes.

22 These numbers are made up for illustrative purposes only. Some apps will cost more to assess, whereas others will cost less—and costs will change over time. In the next chapter, we'll explore how to determine how much you should spend on security.

First, let's consider how these numbers play out on a per-assessment basis. As you can see in this matrix, when client A does assessments only once per year, every assessment costs $100,000. By contrast, when client B is on a six-month reassessment interval, they're paying only $40,000 per assessment (after investing in the initial assessment, of course, which is the same as what client A invested, too).

Comparing Per-Year Costs

	Client A	Client B
Cadence	12 months	6 months
Year 1	$100,000	$140,000
Year 2	$100,000	$80,000
Year 3	$100,000	$80,000
Year 4	$100,000	$80,000
Year 5	$100,000	$80,000
Year 6	$100,000	$80,000

Next, let's consider these numbers on a per-year basis. As this chart demonstrates, when client A invests only once per year in their security assessments, they get an initial assessment every time, and thus their costs are $100,000 per year. By contrast, when client B invests in a six-month interval, they get two assessments at $40,000 each for a total of $80,000 per year. Think about how cool that is; your annual costs go down *because* you're doing security more frequently.

There is of course a temporary spike in year 1 where client B actually is paying more than client A because they're paying for both an initial assessment at $100,000 and a reassessment at

$40,000. However, that $40,000 difference is recouped by year 3, which we can see when we consider how expenses accumulate over time.

Comparing Aggregate Costs over Time

	Client A	Client B
Cadence	12 months	6 months
Year 1	$100,000	$140,000
Year 2	$200,000	$220,000
Year 3	$300,000	$300,000
Year 4	$400,000	$380,000
Year 5	$500,000	$460,000
Year 6	$600,000	$540,000

As you can see here, even despite that temporary increase in year 1 for client B, their long-term investment is lower than client A, even despite getting more regular help on improving the security of their solution.

Comparing Average Costs per Assessment
(Lumping In the Initial Assessment Investment)

	Client A	Client B
Cadence	12 months	6 months
Year 1	$100,000	$70,000
Year 2	$100,000	$55,000
Year 3	$100,000	$50,000
Year 4	$100,000	$47,500
Year 5	$100,000	$46,000
Year 6	$100,000	$45,000

Finally, if you wanted to consider your investment through the lens of an average investment—including the initial assessment—you can see that client B's average assessment cost starts lesser than client A and drops dramatically over time. These numbers consider the total accumulated cost of all assessments and then divide that by the total number of assessments. For example, by year 6, client A has invested in six initial assessments at $100,000 each, for a total of $600,000. Divide that by six, and you get $100,000 each. In the same time frame, client B has invested in one initial assessment at $100,000, and eleven reassessments at $40,000 each. This adds up to $540,000 which, divided by twelve, equals $45,000 each. Remember the candy I mentioned earlier? This is where that concept comes from. Twelve for $5.40 is a much better deal than six for $6.

No matter how you look at it, it's less expensive to do security assessments at the appropriate interval (which is usually more frequent than the common misconception of doing it annually). The ROI is proven out by these numbers. Your CFO will love this; make it part of your case when seeking budget approval.

Security is a lifetime investment; you'll always be working on it. It will not end. So my advice to you is to invest in the initial assessment just once (and only once!), and don't look back. Avoid the trap of waiting too long, which will result in you paying that higher price every time. Get yourself the reassessment price instead. Keep on the appropriate cadence and you'll do more, better, and for less expense.

BENEFIT #3: THE RIGHT CADENCE
DELIVERS BETTER PARTNERSHIP VALUE

When you reassess your app at the proper cadence, you get the best value from your security partner, too. The more they know, the better they can help.

Consider the many decisions you face during the development process: decisions about design, implementation, roadmap, and strategy. Each of those decisions impact security. *Every single one.*

A couple of problems arise when you work with your security partner too infrequently. First, you miss out on their advice at the crucial moments you need it most: when you are making decisions. Second, because you've kept them out of the loop, they usually can't quickly help when you need it on-demand; they need to get up to speed first.

By contrast, when you work with them at appropriate intervals, you're able to more effectively address security when making crucial decisions. Coordinating regularly with your security partner ensures they understand where you are and what's changing. This translates into better ability to help you make good security decisions, including especially when you need it on-demand.

I once received an urgent phone call from the VP of product at a longtime client. He was alarmed about a security certification program that had just been announced in his industry. He assumed his customers would force him to go through it. He feared that the new program might require different security than what he had been doing. If that turned out to be the case, it could mean that pending contracts might not be approved. It could even mean that existing contracts might be canceled. Needless to say, he was worried. He wanted to know what he should do.

Fortunately, his company was on a strict three-month reassessment cadence with us. Because of this regular contact, I understood their product roadmap in intimate detail. I was able to advise him—right there on that unexpected phone call—about how this program would impact him. I was able to advise him on what he should do. Without the insight, familiarity, and transparency that are delivered by regular collaboration, there's no way I could have provided advice like that. Especially not on-demand.

What otherwise would have been a train wreck of uncertainty for him turned into an action plan instead. It took only a few minutes. This outcome was achievable thanks to his more frequent reassessment cadence, which, by the way, also delivered better security that was less expensive, too.

HOW TO KEEP PERSPECTIVES FRESH

It's pretty common to hear people say that they want to change their security partner every year or two in an effort to get "fresh perspectives." The spirit of this makes sense: you want to avoid routines or complacency that would cause blind spots. However, keep in mind that the point is about changing perspectives, not necessarily about changing partners.

There are good reasons to change your security partner. If they're inflexible, hard to work with, or deliver subpar results, you should replace them. Same if they give you bloated and unhelpful reports, rely too heavily on tools rather than manual investigation, or are unable to execute *every* element of the method you learned in chapter 4. Furthermore, even if you aren't *dissatisfied*, but you come across a partner who can *better* achieve your goals, that would be a good reason to change, too. In fact, I'd even go so far as to recommend that you reevaluate your partner right now anyway, given that there are so few security companies who understand (let alone implement) the ideas in this book. That means it's highly likely that you've already hired the wrong partner. If you did, that's a good reason to change, too.

But don't change just for the sake of change. That's inefficient and doesn't necessarily solve your problems anyway.

So how do you change *perspectives* without changing *partners*? Here's how we do it, and I recommend any security partner you hire does the same—because it works:

- **Rotate personnel from project to project.**[23] This cross-pollinates ideas and brings fresh viewpoints learned from other projects. It also cross-trains in ways that make everyone better.

- **Establish continuity.** While analysts rotate between projects, also ensure that at least one analyst is involved with every project, serving as the leader who guides

---

23 The inherent requirement on this one is that your partner would need to have enough skilled analysts to rotate around. Many boutique consulting firms consist of only a few people. Even the big, traditional business-consulting firms usually have only a small number of ethical hackers (if they have any at all). Either way, those headcount constraints impede the ability to deliver this kind of rotation. Make sure you understand size, scope, and breadth of analyst expertise when vetting your partner, as it impacts this specifically.

the team. This ensures that all accumulated knowledge continually delivers efficiency.

- **Transfer knowledge.** Ensure that everyone teaches each other what they know. This not only spreads the expertise but also makes people better; teaching forces a person to understand an idea in different ways. That in itself delivers fresh perspectives.

- **Challenge assumptions.** As analysts rotate into different projects, ensure they challenge ideas and approaches presented by others working on the project. This ensures that everyone's thinking is continually sharpened and improved.

When these things are done right, it not only gives fresh perspectives, but it also delivers two extra benefits. First, it multiplies expertise. For example, we have some people who dominate firmware projects, whereas others dominate cloud projects. Pairing them on various projects makes both of them better at each other's specialty. Second, it protects against turnover. Due to the skills shortage you learned about in chapter 1, security professionals are in high demand, constantly subject to poaching. By rotating personnel and transferring knowledge, it ensures that when someone leaves, the rest of the team is still fully operational and efficient in executing your project.

The key takeaway of this chapter is this: reassessments matter, and you need to do them frequently. That's how you find the flaws, avoid rolling out vulnerable solutions, and keep yourself out of the breach headlines. You keep getting better.

In karate, a black belt is not the end; it's the beginning. Same idea with security. Once you've done your first security assessment, the journey is not over: it's only just begun. Security is a never-ending loop toward excellence. Keep hacking your app in an ongoing cycle of reassessments.

Because if you're good, you're never done.

BIG IDEAS

Do reassessments right so they're more effective, less expensive, and deliver better partnership.

- Change comes in many forms. All of them require you to revisit your security.

- Vulnerabilities continue to appear after the initial assessment. Reassessments ensure you continue to identify them so you can fix them. Reassessments are the lifeblood of your long-term security success.

- For most companies, the right reassessment cadence is every three to six months. If you hit the right cadence, you account for change. If you wait too long, you cede the advantage to your attackers.

- The right cadence is more effective, less expensive, and delivers better partnership value.

- Getting fresh perspectives is important. Ideally, you can achieve this by first hiring the right partner and then rotating personnel within their team. If they should be replaced, then replace them, but otherwise avoid changing partners just for the sake of change.

For downloadable templates, team exercises, and real-world examples, go to *tedharrington.com/hackable*.

Now that you know how to approach reassessments, let's explore how to spend your limited money and time. You don't want to invest too much or too little. You want to get it "just right."

CHAPTER 7

SPEND WISELY

LIE
Security is expensive.

TRUTH
You get what you pay for.

Goldilocks knows what's up.

You've heard the fable: she goes for a walk in the woods and comes upon a house. In the house, she finds three bowls of porridge. The first is too hot, the second is too cold, but the third is just right.

Goldilocks is the master of figuring out "just right." You need to be, too.

When it comes to application security, there is too much effort, too little effort, and then the sweet spot that is *just right*.

*Balance effort and risk to guide
your security investment.*

THE GOLDILOCKS PRINCIPLE

The Goldilocks principle is the idea that you can invest too much or too little in trying to find vulnerabilities, but what you need to do is find the best balance.

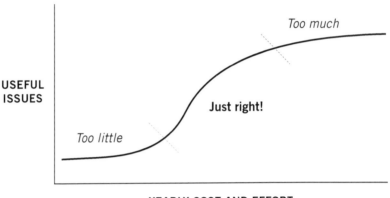

TOO MUCH EFFORT

Is it possible to invest *too much* effort in your security?

Yup.

At a certain point, you start to see diminishing returns: issues still appear but more rarely. Security is never really "done," so it's tricky knowing when to move on. There's always more to do, more to find, more to fix. Knowing when to wrap up depends on your threat model, risk appetite, and your unique circumstances.

However, you probably aren't in this category anyway. Almost nobody is. In all the years we've been doing this, and in all the years my friends have been doing this, I can count only one company who ever hit this inflection point all on their own. *One!*

But you certainly *can* get there. The takeaway is this: security is *not* an endless investment of resources. There *is* a point at which you can accept the remaining risk and move forward.

TOO LITTLE EFFORT

Almost everyone falls into this category.

Security is often viewed as a "tax" on the business. Companies want to minimize any kind of tax, and so they try to cut security costs. However, most people don't realize that when you cut *costs*, what you actually cut is *effort*: how much time you invest, how manual it is, how much attack surface you cover, and how thoroughly you develop custom exploits. That's a dangerous elixir because your attackers already invest more effort than you can. Cutting effort just cedes more advantage.

Price is an incredibly important factor in any decision. However, you shouldn't lose focus on *outcomes*. Let's imagine you need to get from New York to Los Angeles. The best way to get there is on a commercial airline. You'll be there in a few hours for a few hundred dollars. There is a cheaper option, though: Rollerblades. Like a seat on a commercial flight, Rollerblades are indeed a mode of transportation. Better yet, they're way less expensive, too.

But that's stupid.

Although Rollerblades *appear* less expensive, they *actually* incur tremendous cost in other ways. Neither your body nor the Rollerblades are built for that kind of journey. It would take months instead of hours. The likelihood of reaching your destination is close to zero.

This absurdity is exactly what it's like to underinvest in your security mission. You make it harder, take longer, and feel awful along the way. You torpedo your chances of success. Despite being an obviously bad approach, people pursue this line of thinking *all the time*.

If that sounds like you, I feel your pain. You're under tremendous pressure to make the best use of the limited money and person-power you have, and those resources need to cover a wide range of priorities. It's sometimes hard to justify the investment in security, and even when you can, you aren't always sure where the best place to invest it might be. Others in the business sometimes don't even understand security, so trying to get their approval is like shouting into the wind. As a result, decisions sometimes are made on price tag alone, without adequate consideration of the impact this has on your ability to succeed.

Here's the harsh reality, though: the less you invest, the less it returns. When you cut costs too far, you prevent outcomes that help you get better. Achieving your security mission is going to cost you time, effort, and money. There is no way around that. When those investments get cut to the bone, what's *really* reduced is your ability to succeed.

THE LEVEL OF EFFORT THAT'S "JUST RIGHT"

The trick lies in finding your sweet spot, that magical balance where you uncover useful issues without investing too much or too little. There are many variables that influence this, including:

- The value of your assets

- The skills of your adversaries

- The scope of your attack surfaces

- The amount of risk you're willing to accept

We'll explore these variables when discussing threat modeling in the next chapter, but for now, just understand this: application security testing is probably going to cost $30,000–$150,000+ per year, per application.[24] Some cost far more than that.

That number may shock you. If you're used to paying $25,000, $10,000, or even less than $5,000 per year for security testing, you're probably doing vulnerability scanning alone. You're pulling on Rollerblades to try to get across the country.

So why is a price tag like this even necessary? A few reasons.

First, doing it right isn't easy. It takes effort. As much as the marketers want you to believe that security can be easy, quick, and cheap, it simply isn't. An athlete can't make the varsity team just because she does some push-ups now and then; she needs to dedicate the time, effort, and passion to achieve her goal. That's how building better, more secure software works, too.

Second, the incremental cost of doing security right is a tiny, microscopic spec compared to the gigantic cost of a security incident. Security breaches are expensive. Between paying top

---

24 These figures are valid as of the time of publishing. However, as with anything involving money: inflation, changing market conditions, and other economic factors will cause these to increase over time.

dollar for incident response, potential fines, hits to your revenue, reduction in your stock value (if you are publicly traded), and the long road to earning back customer trust—the exposure runs into the millions of dollars in most cases. In some cases, it has even put companies out of business.

Third, security is a competitive advantage. Once you've improved the security of your solution, you can prove it to your customers. Your competitors who fail to do security right are unable to match you, which makes you look like the better choice. Your customers become more comfortable, smoothing the path to sales. Better yet, if you're effective in earning their trust (which I'll teach you how to do in chapter 10), you might even be able to charge a price premium.

Nevertheless, you may be wondering: how do you get the comprehensive assessment you need but for the cheap price you want?

Well, you can't.

You can't achieve security excellence by going cheap. You can't find the unknowns for cheap. You can't discover custom exploits for cheap. You get what you pay for, and there's no way around that.

However, that's not even the right question to be asking. Instead, ask *this* question: Do you *need* a comprehensive assessment—performed by an external expert—or is something less rigorous acceptable?

That, my friend, depends on your risk tolerance. Once you know how much risk you're willing to accept, you can invest accordingly.

The cost is the cost; it's the *effort* that is variable. And effort is based on risk.

RISK → EFFORT → COST

When you invest only in cheap security approaches, you accept the risk of all of the vulnerabilities you leave undiscovered. Remember, your vulnerabilities exist. The question is simply whether you *fix* them or attackers *exploit* them.

Risk is a field unto itself, and discussing how to calculate it is beyond the scope of this book.[25] However, it's worth a quick introduction to the concept.

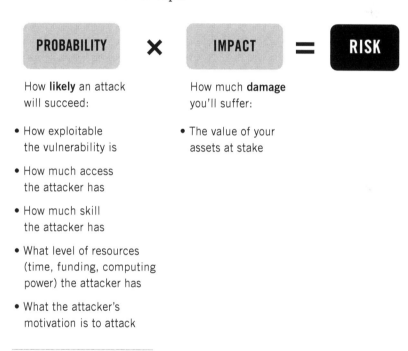

PROBABILITY ✕ **IMPACT** = **RISK**

How **likely** an attack will succeed:

- How exploitable the vulnerability is
- How much access the attacker has
- How much skill the attacker has
- What level of resources (time, funding, computing power) the attacker has
- What the attacker's motivation is to attack

How much **damage** you'll suffer:

- The value of your assets at stake

---

25 For deeper analysis on calculating risk, check out ISACA, a prominent organization that serves audit professionals. Here is a good place to start: Shubhamangala B. R. and Snehanshu Saha, "Application Security Risk: Assessment and Modeling," *ISACA Journal* 2 (March 2016), https://www.isaca.org/Journal/archives/2016/volume-2/Pages/application-security-risk.aspx.

Once you've computed these variables, you can quantify risk. Then you decide how much risk you're willing to accept. Use *that* to decide how much to spend. Risk drives the amount of effort you should invest in finding and fixing vulnerabilities. The level of effort drives the cost of your security investment.

Risk drives effort. Effort drives cost.
Don't do it the other way around.

❌ RISK ⟵ EFFORT ⟵ COST

Don't let cost drive your risk decisions. When you start with cost and try to reduce it, you actually reduce effort. When you reduce effort, you increase the risk you accept.

There's no way around that simple reality. When you lead with cost, you let the wrong factors drive your security mission. Instead, use the right factors to drive your security mission: what you want to protect, why, and from whom.

YOU GET WHAT YOU PAY FOR

It's harsh, but you know it's true. You get what you pay for.

This is usually framed as a negative: buy something cheap, and it will fail. It's like when you buy the cheap version of a power tool, which quickly breaks. Then you replace it with the more expensive version you should've bought in the first place.

However, there's an equally positive frame as well: invest in the *right* thing, and you obtain the *right* outcome. Buy the right power tool the first time, and you get the project done right.

Either way, you get what you pay for.

EFFORT DRIVES LIKELIHOOD OF DISCOVERY

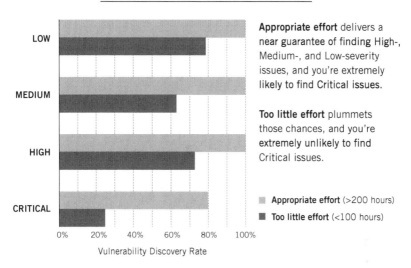

Appropriate effort delivers a near guarantee of finding High-, Medium-, and Low-severity issues, and you're extremely likely to find Critical issues.

Too little effort plummets those chances, and you're extremely unlikely to find Critical issues.

▨ **Appropriate effort** (>200 hours)
▰ **Too little effort** (<100 hours)

Here are some powerful data points about effort, extracted from two years of our security assessments:

- Investing *more* than 200 hours in a security assessment results in high-, medium-, and low-severity issues almost 100 percent of the time. Critical vulnerabilities are discovered more than 80 percent of the time.

- Investing *less than* 100 hours in a security assessment drops those success metrics sharply. Critical vulnerabilities are discovered less than 25 percent of the time.

Here's the point: *effort drives outcomes.*

The only difference between these two data points is the level of effort invested. The vulnerabilities exist either way. Given that you want to find your vulnerabilities so you can fix them, this data *begs* you to invest the amount of effort that actually drives that outcome.

To put these numbers in context, vulnerability scanning falls well under 100 hours of effort (many even under ten hours). By contrast, manual white-box vulnerability assessments quickly climb over 200 hours. If you truly want to find and fix your vulnerabilities, you need to put in the effort to find them. If you do, you will. If you don't, you won't.

EFFORT DRIVES VOLUME OF VULNERABILITIES

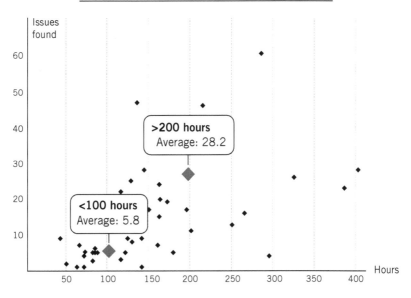

Not only does the *likelihood* of finding issues increase as the effort increases, but so too does the *volume*.

- Investing *more than* 200 hours in a security assessment delivers an average of 28.2 vulnerabilities.

- Investing *less than* 100 hours in a security assessment delivers an average of 5.8 vulnerabilities.

There's that simple truth, yet again: *effort drives outcomes*.

Think about that for a moment: if your system has twenty-eight vulnerabilities, but you only invest in finding five of them, what do you achieve? Maybe you save a little money in the short term. Maybe that makes your CFO happy. But you also accept massive risk. You leave yourself exposed. You concede the advantage to your attacker. You set yourself up for bigger expenses later if there's a security incident.

Let's put these numbers in context, too: these are unique, verified vulnerabilities, with customized severity ratings that make sense in the context of your architecture and threat model. That's massively different from what vulnerability scanners produce: hundreds of findings that are mostly just the same issue repeated, fail to calibrate severity to your unique scenario, and include tons of false positives.

In any event, consider reframing your budget discussions: speak in terms of *vulnerabilities* in addition to speaking in terms of *dollars*. For example, instead of only asking for "$50,000," ask for "twenty vulnerabilities" as well. That completely reframes the conversation to the entire point of security testing: find your security flaws before your attackers do. The budget approvers might still say no, but at least they'd understand what they're saying no to.

If you allocate appropriate effort, you *will* find vulnerabilities. That means you *will* be able to fix them. That means you *will* get better. This data demonstrates that there is a threshold of effort required to do that. If you invest too little, outcomes will diminish. But if you invest appropriately instead, you set yourself up to succeed.

THERE'S NO "ONE SIZE FITS ALL" BUDGET

I advise a group of technology executives who often ask each other how much to spend on security. They usually suggest problematic answers to each other. For example, one CTO recommended a budget of $1,000/year. *One thousand dollars!* To defend against nation-states, organized crime, hacktivists, corporate espionage, casual hackers, accidental insiders, disgruntled insiders, opportunistic insiders, and malicious insiders. What are the chances he succeeds with that budget?

Zero.

By contrast, another CTO recommended a budget of over $1,000,000/year. Her chances are definitely better than if her budget was only $1,000/year. But is it appropriate for her peers? Is it even appropriate for her? I don't know. The only way to answer that is: "it depends." Conditions vary widely. There's simply not a budget that works for everybody.

However, there *are* some universal truths:

1. Not all applications are created equal.

2. Not all applications share the same risk profile.

3. Not all applications warrant the same level of effort or spending.

4. There is a minimum effort you need to invest.

Some applications require heavy investment. Others are OK with less. Maybe your assets are of low value, and $30,000 for an assessment is fine. Or maybe your attack surface is vast, and $150,000 barely scratches the surface. Determining which group you fall into depends on how much risk you face, how much of it you want to reduce, and how much you're willing to accept. You've got to find your own "just right."

Your investment depends on a variety of factors, including:

- **Size** of your company, in-house security team, and software development project

- **Value** of your assets

- **Amount** of effort you've already invested in security, your tolerance for risk, your customer's tolerance for risk, and the security sophistication in your industry

- **Conditions**, such as regulatory requirements that you must comply with, the capabilities of your in-house security team, the scope of your application's attack surfaces, and the frequency at which you update your software

As you learned earlier in this chapter, you're going to spend between $30,000 and $150,000+ on security testing, per application, per year. Almost everyone who achieves security excellence invests in this range. However, most companies invest far less than this.

FACTORS THAT INFLUENCE YOUR SECURITY BUDGET

SIZE
- Your company
- Your internal security team
- Your software development project

VALUE
- Your assets

CONDITIONS
- Regulatory requirements
- In-house security capabilities
- Scope of attack surfaces
- Update frequency

AMOUNT
- Effort already invested in security
- Your risk tolerance
- Your customers' risk tolerance
- Security sophistication in your industry

Your budget goes beyond just testing, though. An effective security process also includes:

- Salary, benefits, and overhead associated with your in-house security personnel

- Salary, benefits, and overhead associated with your in-house nonsecurity personnel, prorated by the amount of time they spend on security

- Effort by your developers in dealing with remediations of security vulnerabilities

- Training, certifications, and other professional development for your security staff

- Overhead to manage the security process, both internally and externally

- Security software, products, and tool licenses

You can assume that security consulting and testing will consume anywhere from 20–50 percent of your overall security budget, with the above categories consuming the other 50–80 percent.

With those in mind, here are some ways to think about your overall application security budget. Don't use these to *set* your budget but rather as a litmus test. If these sound like you, you're nailing "just right." If you're far off from these, it means you need to rethink your investments.

BUDGET METHOD #1: BY DEVELOPMENT BUDGET

One benchmarking method is to consider your application security budget as a ratio of your overall software development budget. It's a relative percentage that decreases as your overall budget increases. For example:

Overall Development Budget (Per Year)	Percent for Security	Overall Security Budget (Per Year)
$1,000,000	30 percent	$300,000
$2,000,000	24 percent	$480,000
$4,000,000	19 percent	$760,000
$8,000,000	15 percent	$1,200,000
$16,000,000	12 percent	$1,920,000
$32,000,000	10 percent	$3,200,000

BUDGET METHOD #2: BY TEAM SIZE

Another way to benchmark your security budget is to consider it in the context of your overall software development team. As the team grows, the amount you budget for security grows, too. For example:

Product Team Headcount (Excluding Salespeople)	Overall Security Budget (Per Year)
5	$300,000
10	$500,000
20	$850,000
40	$1,350,000
80	$2,050,000
160	$3,000,000
320	$4,250,000

BUDGET METHOD #3: BY REVENUE

A third litmus test to benchmark your security budget would be to think about it in terms relative to your top-line revenue. As revenue increases, the percentage that is allocated to security decreases. For example:

Revenue (Per Year)	Percent for Security	Overall Security Budget (Per Year)
$2,000,000	20 percent	$400,000
$4,000,000	16 percent	$640,000
$8,000,000	13 percent	$1,040,000
$16,000,000	10 percent	$1,600,000
$32,000,000	8 percent	$2,560,000
$64,000,000	7 percent	$4,480,000
$128,000,000	6 percent	$7,680,000

Just keep in mind that all of these benchmarking methods are simply guidelines. They won't work for everyone every time. Some of these might even conflict with each other in your case. The only accurate way to establish your budget is by understanding your unique circumstances. The best way to achieve that is to do each of the following, in partnership with your external security expert:

- **Establish** your threat model (which you'll learn how to do in the next chapter)

- **Use** it to understand your risk scenario, and

- **Determine** how much effort it takes to reduce that risk

When Goldilocks tried that porridge, she found her "just right." You can, too. Ignore the noise: you shouldn't aim for "cheap," nor should you spend endlessly. Both are nonsense. Instead, trust that there is a happy balance that sets you up for success on your security mission, while meeting the financial constraints that exist in every business. Go find that balance.

BIG IDEAS

Balance effort and risk to guide your security investment.

- The Goldilocks principle is the idea that you can invest too much or too little in trying to find vulnerabilities, but what you need to do is find the best balance.
  - Too much effort leads to diminishing returns.
  - Too little effort leaves you exposed; you accept tremendous risk.
  - The right level of effort uncovers useful issues without investing too much or too little.

- Risk drives effort; effort drives cost. Not the other way around.

- Effort drives outcomes. You get what you pay for.

- There is no "one size fits all" budget. Use your overall development budget, overall software development team size, or top-line revenue as a litmus test to benchmark where your security budget should land. If you're very far off, reconsider your investments.

For downloadable templates, team exercises, and real-world examples, go to *tedharrington.com/hackable*.

Now let's talk about your attackers. You need to establish your threat model.

CHAPTER 8

ESTABLISH YOUR THREAT MODEL

LIE

We take security seriously.

TRUTH

*We need to understand the battle
before we can fight it.*

I was in a narrow alley, staring into the eyes of a massive bull. He was charging at full speed.

Worst of all, I put myself in this position. Voluntarily.

This happened during the infamous Running of the Bulls, an event in Pamplona, Spain, where the general public—including knuckleheads like me—put themselves directly in the path of some pissed-off bulls. And then try to run away from them.

Absurd, I know.

You're probably aware that bulls are huge, have razor-sharp horns, and are very angry. There was something I didn't know, though: bulls are fast. *Ridiculously* fast. Way faster than me.

So there I was, staring down this charging bull. As he neared, I jogged over to a fence to climb to safety. Still unaware of his speed, I thought I had plenty of time.

As I climbed the fence, two things alerted me that something was amiss: first, the look of sheer terror on my friend's face, followed instantly by the hot *whoosh* of air as the charging bull ran directly under me, rocking his head upward trying to gore me.

That was a close call. I had grossly misjudged the bull, his speed, and my own safety. I learned a crucial lesson that day:

Understand your situation.

I didn't understand the strengths of the threat (bulls are fast). I didn't understand my own strengths in context of the threat (it doesn't matter how fast I am relative to other humans; I'm pretty slow compared to a charging bull). I didn't adequately prioritize the things I wanted to protect (my physical safety). I didn't consider where the threat might harm me (in my butt, as the bull runs underneath me). And I didn't consider what motivates the threat (bulls compete to establish dominance atop the social structure of a herd; hence they're very aggressive).

As it applies to bulls, so too does it apply to your security mission. You need to understand these same things in order to secure your software. You need to understand your attackers, their motivation, their strengths, what you have that they'd want, and where they'll attack you to get it.

Establishing a threat model is how you do all of this.

Understand what to protect, whom to defend
against, and where you'll be attacked.

WHAT'S A THREAT MODEL?

THREAT MODEL COMPONENTS

ASSETS

ATTACK SURFACES

ATTACKERS
Also known as "Threats," hence "Threat Modeling"

Threat modeling is an adversary-centric exercise in which you define three things:

1. **Assets.** What do you need to protect?

2. **Attackers.** Whom do you need to defend against?

3. **Attack surface.** Where will you be attacked?

These lay the foundation of your entire security plan. They guide where you invest time, effort, and money. You do not have unlimited resources, so you cannot defend against everything all of the time.

You simply cannot win without this plan. As Warren Buffett famously said, "An idiot with a plan can beat a genius without a plan."

Establishing your threat model is a collaborative process between in-house staff and your security partner. In theory, you could develop it all on your own. Or alternatively, you could off-load it entirely to your partner. But it's really better to approach this together. There are many threat modeling frameworks out there, and each has its own merits. The point isn't to compare and contrast the different frameworks. The point is to get super clear on what matters to your company and why in order to determine how to protect it.

Here's an approach that works really well (which is why we use it): we start with a collaborative discussion with our customers about what they need to protect, which informs our thinking about adversaries and attack scenarios. Those then guide how we think about the various attack surfaces we will explore in the security assessment. As a result, our reports briefly describe the assets that the customer noted as important and then briefly describe the adversaries relevant to those assets. Discussion of attack surfaces is then woven into the vulnerability write-ups throughout the report.

Your threat model documentation could be as extensive as a full-blown, stand-alone document that is dozens of pages long, or it could be as simple as an informal summary of the primary components. Either way, the point is less about *documentation* and more about *understanding*. You need to understand your threat model. You simply cannot skip that. Everything you do—from rating severity to prioritizing remediations to communicating to your customers—is all based on the unique circumstances of your threat model.

As far as *when* to do this, the best time is at the beginning of your security journey. In the next chapter, you'll learn how to build security into the development process—establishing a threat model is an action you'll be advised to take during the early stages. However, most people overlook this until much later in the process (and many don't even do it at all, because they didn't even know what a threat model was, let alone why they should have one). If that's your case, that's OK. It's never too late to understand your threat model. Just start working on it now. Furthermore, it's a constantly evolving concept, so you're going to be updating it periodically anyway.

In *The Art of War*, Sun Tzu famously proclaimed the secret to success in battle:

"Know thy enemy. Know thyself."

By establishing your threat model, you do both. You identify and prioritize your attackers. That's how you "know thy enemy." You identify and prioritize your assets and your attack surfaces. That's how you "know thyself." Taken together, you're ready to prioritize your investments of time, effort, and money.

Let's get started.

PART I: KNOW THY ENEMY

It's called "threat modeling" because it's focused on attackers, who are also known as threats.

Attacker motivation is critical to understand. Different adversaries attack for different reasons. You must know *why* they attack so you can know *how* to defend. For example, some attackers want to make money. If your security measures make it too expensive for them to attack you, they'll attack someone else instead.

Common attacker motivations include:

- **Profit**: they want to make money

- **Notoriety**: they want to make a name for themselves

- **Challenge**: they want to prove they can do it

- **Geopolitical gain**: they want to advance their nation's agenda

- **Advocacy**: they want to highlight a cause

- **Competitive advantage**: they want to get an edge over a rival

- **Revenge**: they want to retaliate for a real or perceived injustice

- **Terrorism**: they want to instill fear

- **Espionage**: they want to obtain secrets

- **Economic warfare**: they want to advance their own financial position and weaken a rival's financial position

There's an interesting wrinkle about motivation: even if it's not immediately obvious why, you actually might be the ideal candidate for an attacker to target. For example, consider when one hundred thousand cheap, basic surveillance cameras were attacked and exploited in the Mirai botnet. Neither the small business owners who bought them nor the manufacturers who produced them thought anyone would care to attack these cameras. Yet, it happened. A botnet is a network of compromised devices that are infected and controlled as a group without the owners' knowledge. The Mirai botnet was used in an attack that made the internet unusable for substantial portions of the East Coast of the United States. This was massively disruptive. It made many online services and applications unusable. The motivation wasn't about hurting the store owners. It was about taking the internet offline. The point is this: when you consider why they might attack, you have to think bigger than what's most immediately obvious. Earlier, you learned how and why to think like an attacker; here's when you especially want to apply that advice.

Once you've considered motivation, consider capabilities and why they matter:

- **Skill**. The more talented they are, the more sophisticated their attacks will be.

- **Time**. The more time they dedicate, the more likely they'll succeed.

- **Funding**. The more money they have, the more they can invest in tools, people, and capabilities.

- **Computing resources**. The more processing power, bandwidth, and storage they have, the more effective their attacks will be.

- **Attack resources**. The likelihood they'll succeed skyrockets if they have access to the internet backbone (the array of high-speed networks that enable computer-to-computer traffic over the internet) or stockpiles of zero-day vulnerabilities.

Some attackers have nearly infinite amounts of several of these. Others have almost none. Understanding who has what helps you understand how dangerous your enemies are.

The key to all of this is an important lesson you learned at the beginning of this book: *to defend against attackers, you need to think like them.* I'll explain each attacker type and then prompt you to think about whether you need to worry about them. The prompt questions are not exhaustive—I could fill an entire book with the many wild and crazy attack scenarios that exist (and frankly, it would be really fun to do that! Maybe for my next book). Instead, think of these prompt questions as the start of a discussion. Use them to spark the dialogue among your team as you strive to think like an attacker. Definitely involve your security partner with this element (ideally, they should be driving it).

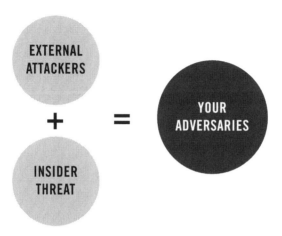

Attackers fall into two primary categories: external attackers and the insider threat. Let's explore each.

OVERVIEW: EXTERNAL ATTACKERS

External attackers don't have any special privileges or access. There are five types: casual hacker, hacktivists, corporate espionage, organized crime, and nation-states.

Casual Hacker

Skill | Time | Funding | Computing Resources | Attack Resources
●●○   ●●●   ●○○   ●○○   ●○○

Casual hackers (also known as individual hackers or small-group hackers) are explorers, problem solvers, and even anarchists. They see hacking as a challenge. They might not even be malicious. They just want to prove they can do it.

San Francisco drivers once saw digital construction signs along the freeway declaring: *"Godzilla attack! Turn back!"*

Of course, this was not an actual warning. It was the result of an attack (just not one from Godzilla). Casual hackers had broken the authentication on the ubiquitous digital signs and changed the display message. They did it as a prank. They did it to prove they could.

To determine if you should concern yourself with this attacker, ask yourself:

- Do you have a prominent brand? If so, a casual hacker would want to brag about exploiting you. Your fame becomes transferable to them if they're successful.

- Do you have a "cool" technology? If you make something cutting edge, newsworthy, or with a strong fan base, a casual hacker might want to brag about hacking it. Your "cool" factor is transferable to them.

- Could you be used in a stunt? Like the roadside construction signs, if there's a fun way to pull a prank, a casual hacker may want to attack your technology.

Hacktivists

Skill	Time	Funding	Computing Resources	Attack Resources
◉◉○	◉◉◉	◉○○	◉◉○	◉○○

Hacktivists have an ideology and attack in order to draw attention to it. This group includes terrorists who pursue ruthless causes.

When the United States Federal Communications Commission (FCC) voted to repeal a polarizing law around net neutrality, the hacktivist collective known as Anonymous disagreed with the controversial reversal. In retribution, they attacked FCC information systems. They did it to take a political stand and highlight their cause.

To determine if you should concern yourself with this attacker, ask yourself:

- Do you have a prominent brand? If so, a hacktivist can obtain media exposure for their mission because a security breach of a prominent brand is newsworthy.

- Is your business controversial or politicized? If so, hacktivists who hold the opposing view may want to attack to advocate for their ideology.

- Are any of your key executives publicly outspoken about polarizing beliefs? Like it or not, the personal beliefs of key executives become reflections of the company. If those beliefs are polarizing, hacktivists who share opposing views may attack for ideological reasons.

Corporate Espionage

Skill	Time	Funding	Computing Resources	Attack Resources
●●●	●●○	●●●	●●○	●●○

Some companies attack each other to gain a competitive advantage, steal intellectual property, or save on research and development (R&D). They have significant budgets and hire elite talent. There's usually a foreign element to this, where a company of one nation attacks companies from another nation. However, domestic examples appear as well.

Chris Correa was an executive for the Saint Louis Cardinals who found a way to access the databases of a rival team. He obtained scouting reports, players' medical histories, and contract negotiation details. The attack went on for years. Professional baseball is enormously competitive, and the unfair advantage he obtained is immeasurable. The punishment, however, was quite measurable: The Cardinals were forced to send $2 million and their top two picks in the next draft to the rival team. Correa himself was sentenced to forty-six months in jail and banned from baseball for life.

To determine if you should concern yourself with this attacker, ask yourself:

- Do you protect valuable information or other assets? If so, this attacker might want to obtain the competitive advantage you possess.

- Do you protect valuable intellectual property in development? If so, this attacker could save time and money by stealing it in order to accelerate their own R&D.

- Do you hold the dominant competitive position in your marketplace? If so, this attacker might want to chip away at your advantage in order to increase their own competitive position.

Organized Crime

Skill	Time	Funding	Computing Resources	Attack Resources
●●●	●●●	●●●	●●○	●●●

Organized criminals want to make money. They have extensive financial resources, dedicate lots of time, acquire elite skills, and have access to stockpiles of zero-days. They're among the most capable adversaries you'll face.

When people across the planet started dying from the coronavirus (COVID-19), a group called The Maze Team attacked Texas's Affordacare Urgent Care Clinic. In the middle of the global pandemic, they encrypted systems and files crucial to the delivery of care, making those systems unusable. Medical staff couldn't treat patients in need of care. The attackers demanded a ransom to unlock the systems so medical staff could get back to treating patients. This demonstrates that profit is an incredibly strong motivator, even when it could literally cost lives.

To determine if you should concern yourself with this attacker, ask yourself:

- Do you need access to your data or operational capabilities every minute, without exception? If so, this attacker might attack in ways that prevent the availability of services in order to force you to pay quickly to avoid downtime.

- Do you protect valuable data or intellectual property that has monetary value to other companies, governments, or groups? If so, this attacker might want to steal those assets in order to monetize them.

- Is your company publicly traded? If so, this attacker might take a short position on your stock and then attack in order to drive the stock price down when the news breaks of your security breach. (Short positions make money when stock value declines.) Alternatively, they might attack to read your earnings reports before they're made public in order to make lucrative trades based on what those reports will do to your stock value.

Nation-States

Skill	Time	Funding	Computing Resources	Attack Resources
●●●	●●●	●●●	●●●	●●●

Nation-states are the most capable and dangerous attacker type there is. They are countries who seek geopolitical advantage. They have tremendous resources, including plenty of money, skill, and computational power. They have access to the internet backbone as well as stockpiles of zero-days. They have nearly unlimited time.

Consider NotPetya, a strand of malware used in one of the most devastating cyberattacks of all time, which experts widely attribute to Russia's intelligence services. Certain properties of the malware suggest that the motive was destruction, primarily aimed at Russia's rival Ukraine, where more than 80 percent of the initial victims were located. The attack spread rapidly, shutting down or outright destroying operations for businesses all over the globe, including Maersk, FedEx, and Mondelez. Total damages are estimated at over $10 billion worldwide.

Many companies assume that a nation-state would not focus on them. That is flawed thinking, though. To determine if you should concern yourself with this attacker, ask yourself:

- Do you collect information that would be beneficial to a rival nation-state (such as location tracking, usage behaviors, or other data about the people of your own nation)? If so, nation-state actors might want this information to inform their financial, political, and other strategies as they compete against your nation.

- Are you involved with critical infrastructure, such as delivery of medical care, power, water, emergency services, food supply, manufacturing, public health, cybersecurity, or any other basic needs of your nation? If so, a nation-state actor may want to disrupt these services, either as a stand-alone attack or in conjunction with a physical attack.

OVERVIEW: THE INSIDER THREAT

Almost every day, I hear someone boast about their security-testing program being awesome because they do "external penetration testing." You've probably heard people say this, too, and maybe you even think it yourself. Here's the problem, though: attackers aren't always coming from an external vantage point. If that's all you're considering, you're already sunk. What about

the external attacker who has escalated privileges and now has insider access? What about the attacker who *is* an insider? What about the people you already know and trust?

External is not enough. You need to look inside, too.

So let's talk about the insider threat.

Many people think that an insider is an employee. That is often true. However, being an insider is not about *employment status*; it's about having elevated *trust* and elevated *access*. Elevated trust means *this* person is trusted more than *other* people. There is confidence that this person will not harm the company. Elevated access means *this* person can access more systems and more assets than *other* people. This person was hired to perform a job and provided the means to do it.

Insiders have these conditions; external attackers do not. All employees have these conditions, of course. However, other trusted parties do, too. Your vendors, third-party integration partners, consultants, advisors, board members, janitors, shareholders, and maybe even your family members can all become the insider threat.

Finally, keep in mind that the insider threat is not a *single type* of attacker. It's a *collection* of attackers, each of which have different motivations, skills, and access to resources. There are four types: accidental insider, opportunistic insider, disgruntled insider, and malicious insider.

Accidental Insider

Skill	Time	Funding	Computing Resources	Attack Resources
●○○	●○○	●○○	●○○	●○○

Accidental insiders are otherwise trustworthy and don't mean to harm your company—they just do something dumb. Even the smartest people click malicious links, download malicious attachments, give up passwords, and plug in USB devices.

Barbara Corcoran, the real estate mogul and star of the TV show *Shark Tank*, once received an invoice for more than $388,000. Assuming it was a legitimate expense related to one of her construction projects, she authorized the invoice and wired the money. However, it didn't go to a contractor working on her project. It went to scammers. Thus, she became an accidental insider. Accidental insiders are actually victims, too, but they are nevertheless the source of your breach.

This matters to every company because humans frequently do dumb things.

Opportunistic Insider

Skill	Time	Funding	Computing Resources	Attack Resources
●●○	●○○	●○○	●○○	●○○

Opportunistic insiders are motivated to obtain some personal gain if—*and only if*—they think they can get away with it. They don't set out to harm your company, but if a good opportunity arises, they'll try.

X-Men Originals: Wolverine leaked before its theatrical release. Fox estimated damages to be in the tens of millions of dollars. It was leaked by Gilberto Sanchez, an insider whose motives *The New York Times* described as to "get props in the movie-loving community...He was scared, but did not imagine he would be blamed."[26] In that single sentence, the newspaper succinctly described the opportunistic insider.

This attacker matters to every company because you must provide access to insiders, and they may attack if they think they can get away with it.

Disgruntled Insider

Skill	Time	Funding	Computing Resources	Attack Resources
●●○	●○○	●○○	●○○	●●○

Disgruntled insiders are motivated by revenge. They start as loyal people, but then something changes. Maybe they are denied a promotion or a contract or disagree with a stance taken by the CEO. Maybe they simply change their political views. As a result, they become angry and set out to hurt your company. Unlike accidental or opportunistic insiders, disgruntled insiders are malicious.

Ricky Joe Mitchell was a network engineer for the oil and gas company EnerVest when he found out he was about to get fired. He decided to retaliate: he reset the company's servers to their original factory settings and disabled critical systems such as

---

26 Michael Wilson, "Adventures of the 'Wolverine' Leaker," *The New York Times*, January 12, 2010, https://www.nytimes.com/2010/01/13/nyregion/13wolverine.html.

cooling equipment and data replication. EnerVest's business was stalled for more than thirty days, causing damages estimated at well over $1,000,000. Mitchell pled guilty and was sentenced to four years in prison plus $528,000 in fines and restitution.

This attacker matters to every company because it's impossible to keep every insider happy all of the time, and it's difficult to know when they decide to retaliate.

Malicious Insider

Skill	Time	Funding	Computing Resources	Attack Resources
●●●	●●●	●○○	●●○	●●○

Malicious insiders are your most dangerous insiders because they are an agent of one of the external groups we previously discussed. That group's resources are often available to malicious insiders, and they are motivated to harm the company. In some cases, the malicious insiders are already an agent when seeking a job or contract with you; in other cases, they're recruited later.

Greg Chung is a Chinese national who became a naturalized US citizen. He worked as an engineer for Boeing on the US Space Shuttle program for more than twenty years. In that time, he stole more than three hundred thousand sensitive documents about the space shuttle, B-1 bomber, C-17 military cargo plane, F-15 fighter jet, and Chinook 47 and 48 helicopters. Every single document was sent to China. The damage to the United States is impossible to quantify.

This attacker matters to every company because your enemies know that getting an insider is the most effective way to achieve their malicious goals. Worse yet, they know that many companies rely on their misplaced confidence in "external penetration testing," while your attackers want to exploit you from the inside.

PART II: KNOW THYSELF

We talked about *them*, now let's talk about *you*. Let's discuss your assets and your attack surfaces.

ASSETS

"What do you want to protect?"

It's a straightforward question that often stumps people. Rarely is it answered uniformly across a company. However, to be successful in your security mission, you *must*. Everyone at your organization needs to:

(a) understand the *entire* list of assets that matter, and
(b) understand how they rank by priority.

Assets are the things that are valuable to you, to your attacker, or both. They are what you need to protect. Assets come in two forms:

- **Tangible assets**: material things that can be stolen, such as personally identifiable information (PII), customer data, business intelligence, or money.

- **Intangible assets**: conditions that can be undermined, such as system availability, authorized access to the system, integrity of your business model, reputation, or trust.

ASSETS

TANGIBLE	INTANGIBLE
e.g., data, money	e.g., reputation, trust

These are what most people focus on...   *...but don't forget about these!*

People usually think about assets too simplistically. They consider some of their assets but not all of them. They think only of tangible assets but fail to also consider intangible assets.

A CIO recently told me that she has only low-value assets to protect: customer email addresses. She stated that she didn't have anything else worth protecting, not even PII—just email addresses. This struck me as odd and probably incorrect because her company's software handles ticketing for festivals and other events. After asking some clarifying questions, it became clear that she protects much more.

Tickets should give just one person access, but an attacker might want to buy one ticket and bring many friends in with him. Or maybe he wants to buy one ticket but sell it many times to unwitting victims. The ticket must work when the patron presents it, but an attacker might want the system to deny paying customers at the door. The ticketing company depends on event producers trusting them, but if they're compromised in ways that hurt the event producer, they will lose trust along with future contracts.

She needs to deal with all of this. Her concerns should go far beyond just email addresses. Yet she didn't realize it.

That scenario unfolds every day. To succeed in your security mission, you need clarity on what to protect. It may not be immediately obvious to you what those things are.

In every consulting or assessment engagement, we always begin by asking about assets. We don't always use that word, though, because it often blinds people to think only about tangible assets like data.

Instead, we use more outcome-oriented questions to drive at what matters. You should, too. These questions include:

- Why does your business exist?

- Who are your customers?

- What do you provide for these customers?

- Why do they choose to get that from you rather than some other way?

- What do you need to protect?

- Why do you want to protect those things?

- What happens if they are compromised?

- What if an attacker did _____?

- If you could protect only one, and one alone, which asset would it be?

- How would you prioritize the rest?

As you think about your own assets, you need to ask yourself these same questions, too. You need everyone at the company to understand how to answer these the same way. Unfortunately, most companies are unable to do that.

I once volunteered to lead a working group in the travel industry. They wanted to understand the security implications of adopting mobile keys, the applications that turn your smartphone into your hotel room key (rather than using a plastic key card). When the working group started discussing assets, a remarkable lack of consensus was revealed. Some people cared about protecting corporate data. Some people cared about protecting guest data. Some people cared about allowing only the right people into a room while keeping everyone else out. All of these were right answers, but interestingly, not everyone mentioned all of them. Whenever I'd ask someone about assets that they hadn't mentioned, they'd always reply, "Oh yeah, that's important, too." That's why you need to actually spell out what you plan to protect. Different people will be thinking different things. Some people will forget to think about things that are important to them. It happens, but the point is that it's flawed to assume that everyone is thinking the same thing.

Once you articulate the assets you want to protect, you need to get everyone on the same page. Now you can have fruitful discussions about what you want to emphasize protecting and what will get lesser emphasis. Deciding what you want to protect informs where you invest time, effort, and money. It's how you determine risk. It's how you determine what to do about that risk.

ATTACK SURFACES

"Where will you be attacked?"

Attack surfaces are the points where data is transferred or accessed. As the name suggests, it's where you get attacked. For example, when planning for a recent security assessment of a smart lock, our analysts considered all of these various attack surfaces:

- the web app

- the firmware and the various processes, ports, or services running on it

- the interfaces, including Bluetooth and Wi-Fi

- the mobile applications

- the backend, including the database interactions, database permissions, firewall rules, and more

Examples of your application's attack surfaces include:

- **Input fields**: login pages, web forms, contact fields

- **Interfaces**: APIs, admin interfaces, transactional interfaces, libraries

- **Integrations**: third-party systems, cloud deployments, integrations with your other systems

- **Storage**: databases, file systems, local storage

- **Security functionality**: authentication, authorization, cryptography, session management

- And more

Ask yourself this simple question: "Can a person or system interact with the app?" Wherever the answer is yes, you've got attack surfaces.

To illustrate the concept, consider *Hacking Hospitals*, which is security research we published exploring how hackers could hurt or kill patients.[27] Part of the project focused on patient monitors, the bedside devices that report vital signs of patients, including heart rate and oxygen levels. In a simulated attack, we found that an attacker could visit the administrative web interface and bypass authentication. This allowed an attacker to log in without credentials. We then found a way to perform remote code execution, which would allow an attacker to run arbitrary system commands. As a result, we proved that an attacker could control how the patient monitor behaves.

If the attacker triggers false alarms, the medical staff responds. This wastes their time and distracts them from patients who actually need their help. Worse yet, it could result in delivering inappropriate care. That has severe implications on patient safety: imagine a patient without heart troubles being administered the electric paddles to restart his heart. That could be fatal.

----

27 Check it out here: Independent Security Evaluators, "Securing Hospitals," February 23, 2016, https://www.ise.io/hospitalhack/.

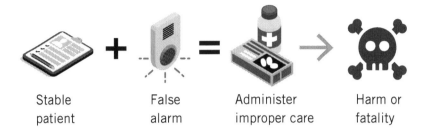

| Stable patient | False alarm | Administer improper care | Harm or fatality |

Conversely, if the attacker silences valid alarms, medical staff does not respond. If a patient who needs care does not get it, the patient suffers or potentially dies. Imagine a patient having a heart attack but not getting the electric paddles to restart her heart. That could be fatal.

| Patient in need of care | Valid alarm disabled | Prevent needed care | Harm or fatality |

In either case, the exploit chain begins at the attack surface of the administrative web interface.

In another simulated attack, we found that the digital kiosks (where you check in for your appointment) could be taken out of kiosk mode (a setting that limits user interaction). This enables an attacker to access other systems on the same network. Shockingly, one such accessible system was the blood work system. From this privileged position, an attacker can change patient blood information. If blood information is wrong, it leads to misdiagnosis or worse, transfusion of the wrong blood type. That is fatal.

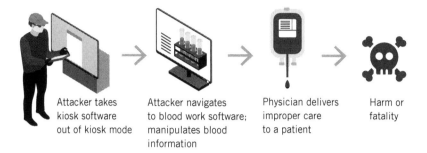

Attacker takes kiosk software out of kiosk mode → Attacker navigates to blood work software; manipulates blood information → Physician delivers improper care to a patient → Harm or fatality

It was assumed that only authorized users could access systems like the blood work software. However, the research demonstrated the opposite. Kiosks are publicly accessible to anyone who visits the hospital, including attackers. From that public vantage point, they can compromise the kiosk software and then manipulate the delivery of care. Literally, any attacker who could physically get to the hospital could do this.

These exploit scenarios demonstrate attack surfaces and how you should think about them.

PART III: IMPLEMENT YOUR THREAT MODEL

Let's tie it all together. Here's what you need to do.

1. **Enumerate your assets.** Develop the list of things you want to protect, and assign value to them.
   - What do you want to protect?
   - What things get you fired if you fail to protect them?
   - What intangible assets have you not considered yet?

2. **Identify your adversaries.** Outline which attackers you're most concerned about and why.

- Who wants your assets? Why do they want them? What's the upside for the attacker?
- How would you force-rank the list of attackers you care most about? Who concerns you most? Least?
- If you focused on defending against just one attacker group and did not focus on any other, would that be acceptable? Why or why not?

3. **Pinpoint your attack surfaces**. Diagram the places where data moves and your adversaries can deploy their attacks in pursuit of your assets.
   - Where can users interact with the system?
   - Where can other systems interact with the system?
   - What third-party integrations, cloud deployments, or dependencies does your system rely on?

4. **Write it down!** Literally write out all of the above. It doesn't need to be fancy, but writing it down delivers three benefits. First, it ensures you consider each fundamental aspect. Second, it reveals discrepancies between what various stakeholders think. Third, it gives you a tool to communicate priorities across the company.

5. **Share it.** Discuss it with leadership, developers, in-house security teams, and your security partners. Make sure everyone is aligned on what you need to protect, from whom, and where you'll be attacked.

To see a real-world example, you can download one at *ted harrington.com/hackable*.

Too many companies stumble on their security mission because they do not understand—let alone implement—this critical element of their defense plan. Don't be one of them. Go take action on this. If you skip your threat model, you don't even know what battle you're in. If you don't know what battle you're in, *you will fail.*

Just like how I eventually understood that speed is what makes a bull dangerous, now you have clarity on how to think about your own attackers. You understand the assets they want to take from you. You understand where they'll attack.

Establish a threat model; it's the foundation of your security plan.

BIG IDEAS

Understand what to protect, whom to defend against, and where you'll be attacked.

- Threat modeling is an adversary-centric exercise in which you define three things: the assets to protect, adversaries to defend against, and attack surfaces where you'll be attacked. It is the foundation of your entire security plan.

- Know thy enemy. Different adversaries attack for different reasons and have different capabilities.
  - External attackers don't have any special privileges or access. There are five types:

casual hacker, hacktivists, corporate espionage, organized crime, and nation-states.
- Insider threats have elevated access and trust. There are four types of insider threats: accidental insider, opportunistic insider, disgruntled insider, and malicious insider.

- Know thyself. Identify and prioritize your assets and your attack surfaces.
    - Assets are the things you want to protect. They're measured in terms of their value to you, or to your attacker, or both. Assets are tangible or intangible. Go beyond just thinking about tangible assets.
    - Attack surfaces are the points where data is transferred or accessed.

- Implement your threat model. If you skip it, you don't even know what battle you're in. If you don't know what battle you're in, *you will fail.*

For downloadable templates, team exercises, and real-world examples, go to *tedharrington.com/hackable.*

Now that you understand the keys to your defense plan, consider how to build security into the development process.

CHAPTER 9

BUILD SECURITY IN

LIE
Develop first, then secure.

TRUTH
Secure as we develop.

Carbon monoxide is colorless, odorless, and tasteless. You don't even know it's there until it kills you. You may be facing your own silent killer: your delay.

I get it: you need to develop and release as fast as possible. You need to measure how the new release performs in the market. You need to see revenue grow. Once you've done all this, *then* you can think about security.

That makes sense. Except it doesn't.

Security is part of what makes a product viable. Your customers expect it. Just like you can't postpone a feature that is core to your value proposition, you can't defer security either. However, if you do it right, you avoid the headache and heartache that otherwise is waiting for you later.

Let me explain with a metaphor. Most mornings, I have a smoothie for breakfast. It's packed with wholesome stuff: organic spinach, bananas, pea protein, cashew butter, and plenty of good ol' H_2O. Once I've poured my smoothie, there are two ways I can clean the blender:

1. **Do it later.** Let it sit in the sink while I rush off to do other urgent things. When I come back later, those nutritious ingredients have hardened and are a pain in the neck to scrub clean. As a result, I have to soak the blender, disassemble it, scrub it, and reassemble it. *or*

2. **Do it now.** As soon as I pour out the smoothie, add a little soap and water into the blender, run it for ten seconds, and rinse. The thing literally cleans itself. No disassembly, no scrubbing.

Doing it later is easier at first but a nightmare overall. Doing it now is easier overall but often dismissed at first.

That's the same scenario you are in as you decide what to do about security. Most people unwittingly pursue the approach that makes their lives harder. Instead, pursue the approach that makes your life easier. If you want to do it the easy way, you need to take action early by building security into the development process. If you don't, you've signed up for the hard way.

> *Build security into the development process: it is more effective and less expensive than delaying security.*

"BUILD SECURITY IN" VS. "BOLT SECURITY ON"

My friend has this incredible roof deck, complete with a grill, big-screen TV, sound system, and amazing views. But it's missing an important element: a permit. When he built the roof deck, my friend skipped that step. He planned to come back to it later. When he tried to sell the house, a buyer's inspection flagged the lack of a permit, which killed the sale. He had to overhaul the work he'd already done on the roof deck. It was expensive. It was infuriating. It took forever. If he had just done it right in the first place, his life would have been so much simpler.

That's what it's like to "bolt security on." Build first, consider security later. That's how most people approach security of their application. The reasons for this are many: there's pressure to meet deadlines, and security is often not viewed as something that's required prior to release. People don't realize it's more expensive and more painful to delay security. There's a misperception that you need to see how the market responds to a release before it's worth trying to secure it.

As with the roof deck, this approach is painful. In a moment, I'll teach you why. But first, let's explore what you should do instead: "build security in." This is when you consider security at each stage of the development process. Some elements you handle in-house, other elements your security partner handles (I'll explain who does what and when). This way, you invest incrementally along the way. It makes your life easier and is less expensive overall. It also ensures that you get security right.

"BUILD SECURITY IN" IS
LESS EXPENSIVE THAN "BOLT SECURITY ON"

Consider that roof deck, and ponder which would've been easier:

1. Buy lumber and hardware that meet code. Install them per code. Get a permit.

2. Buy lumber and hardware that does not meet code. Install them in violation of code. Fail inspection. Tear out old lumber and hardware. Hire a contractor to haul the debris away. Buy new lumber and hardware that meets code. Install new lumber and hardware in ways that meet code. Schedule another inspection. Get a permit.

My friend did the latter. It was a *lot* harder that way. It's the same when you postpone security: you create unnecessary additional work for yourself.

Security done early is less expensive than security done later. This is thanks primarily to avoiding that unnecessary work while you also save on consulting fees. Upon analyzing thirteen years of our own assessment data, we discovered that companies who "built security in" spent 10.1 percent less on consulting fees than those who didn't. That's not a mind-blowing savings, but hey, 10.1 percent is 10.1 percent! That's real money that doesn't go out your door. Why waste it? You might not even realize it, but when you push security off until later, you're taking on that waste. You're making it cost more. This costs more because your security partner has to spend more time and effort (which equates to your money) in addressing a higher volume of security issues than if those security issues had been addressed during the development process first.

Better yet, as cool as it is to save 10.1 percent on consulting fees, that pales in comparison to the savings in terms of *your effort*. It's easiest to fix a flaw at the moment when it's introduced. It's exponentially harder to fix it later. For example, a flaw introduced in the design phase that isn't addressed until after deployment is going to require a ton more effort to fix. In fact, the data shows it takes twenty-five times more effort.

Twenty. Five. Times. More. Effort.

That's bananas!

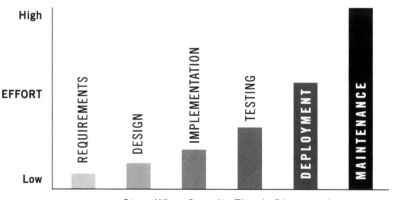

THE LATER YOU SECURE, THE MORE PAINFUL IT BECOMES

Stage When Security Flaw Is Discovered

Unlike consulting fees, these costs are not easily visible on your financial statements. Something that should take one hour now takes twenty-five hours. This is straight-up lost efficiency. You just burned twenty-four additional hours to get the same outcome if you'd just done it earlier.

That's nuts.

When developers are fixing systems they *already built*, they're not working on other things. Salary, benefits, and overhead appear on company financial statements either way; however, developers' *productivity* plummets. This decreases the value the company gets out of each developer. It's a massive hit to your output. If this isn't alarming you, you're not human. No one likes waste, especially when it doesn't improve outcomes.

No rational person wants anything to be twenty-five times harder than it needs to be. Yet, people do this *all the time*. This happens not because people want to make their lives harder; it happens because they don't *realize* it's happening. My mission is to help you stop incurring this waste. Whenever you postpone security, you incur this terrible tradeoff. Every single time.

Introducing vulnerabilities is going to happen—that's a reality of software development (and is the reason that this book exists). But it's hugely inefficient to let them linger in your system any longer than they need to. The book *Applied Software Management* spells out this truth. It explains that (a) most vulnerabilities are introduced during development, but (b) most testing isn't done until after release, yet (c) remediation costs rise exponentially after release.[28]

It's literally that simple: when you delay, it costs you.

You want to shrink that productivity hit. You want to harvest that effort so you can use it for other things instead. When you "build security in," you convert this waste into efficiency. You save effort. You maximize productivity.

---

28 Capers Jones, *Applied Software Management: Assuring Productivity and Quality* (New York: McGraw-Hill, 1996).

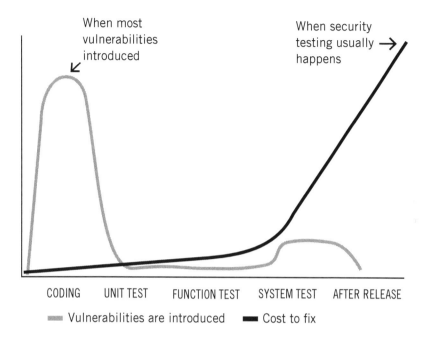

CODING   UNIT TEST   FUNCTION TEST   SYSTEM TEST   AFTER RELEASE

▨▨▨ Vulnerabilities are introduced   ▬ Cost to fix

Graph reproduced and slightly modified for simplicity, with permission from the author.

Perhaps most importantly, this is the best way for a company to take care of its developers. Developers are overloaded, overwhelmed, and hate inefficiency. The last thing they want to do is to revise work they've already done. When that happens, they get frustrated, and it feels like a step backward. However, when you "build security in," you avoid all of that. It's hard to quantify morale boost, but I assure you, developers will love it when inefficiency is removed.

So do yourself a favor and "build security in." If you do, you quickly resolve vulnerabilities as they're introduced, and you might even avoid introducing them altogether. You save effort. You save fees. Developers' lives are much better.

"BUILD SECURITY IN" IS MORE
EFFECTIVE THAN "BOLT SECURITY ON"

When you consider security early and often, it produces better security than if you only consider it later. That point is so straightforward that I debated even mentioning it.

If security is part of every decision, security is part of every result.

If security is not part of every decision, security is not part of every result.

The security of your application suffers when security is not a priority (let alone a consideration). Conversely, when security *is* considered, you position yourself to make good decisions at the very moment that issues are introduced. By considering security at each stage of the development process, it forces you to constantly ask questions such as:

"Does this affect access to assets?"

"How valuable are those assets?"

"Which attackers want those assets?"

"How does this change our threat model?"

"What can we do right now to prevent an attack?"

Every domain in your business—including especially security—requires you to make tradeoffs. You have only limited resources, while many stakeholders compete for those resources. So you have to decide where to best allocate them. To do that, you need to evaluate the pros and cons of a given decision so you can make the right decision at the right time.

But what happens when you ignore a domain of your business? It turns out that you're still making a decision: you simply decide to prioritize other things instead. Let me be abundantly clear about what this means: when security is not considered, you are actively deciding to prioritize other things over security. When that happens, security suffers.

One of our customers had failed to consider rate-limiting during their design phase (which happened before they brought us onto the team). We discovered a nasty exploit as a result. Here's the attack sequence:

1. **Obtain a leaked password database.** Such databases are readily available and usually contain millions of credential pairs. Attackers know that many people (a) don't change passwords and (b) reuse them across services. This means that attackers can assume that at least some credential pairs compromised at one service are likely to grant access to another service.

2. **Write an automated script.** Attempt every credential pair in the leaked password database. Without rate-limiting, the attacker can make an unlimited number of failed attempts in an effort to find valid credentials.

3. **Go to lunch.**

By the time our analyst returned from lunch, he had valid credentials. Not just for any user—for an *admin* user. This gave him the highest level of privilege in the system—he could do anything he wanted to it. It also turns out that the system didn't have multifactor authentication (also known as MFA, the mechanism to prove identity that requires the user to successfully present two or more pieces of evidence before being granted access. You know how some apps text you a code before you can log in? That's MFA). This meant that besides the leaked credential pair, no additional authentication was required to log in as the admin user. Taken together, this meant a complete system compromise. An attacker could own the entire application and do anything they want with it.

If security had been considered during the design phase, these vulnerabilities would have been identified *immediately*. They would have been quickly fixed. They would have delivered a more effective security model during all subsequent phases in the development process. However, because security wasn't considered during the design phase, this catastrophic exploit sequence was introduced. And it was much harder to fix.

By contrast, if you consider security in each stage of the development process, it delivers you a much more effective security model than if you do not. We worked with a different company whose story is much less dramatic but demonstrates the more desirable outcome you want. During the design process, they outlined the intended use case for the system. That quickly led to the suggestion that they implement both rate-limiting and MFA. They did. As a result of that thirty-minute discussion, they avoided introducing this same type of systemwide compromise. It goes without saying: that was far more effective in delivering security by building it into the design process. And it cost them less—both in terms of our fees and in terms of their effort to fix the issues.

Legendary boxer Muhammad Ali famously said, "What you're thinking, you're becoming." If you're constantly thinking about security, you're becoming secure.

HOW TO "BUILD SECURITY IN"

Now that you've explored *why* to build security into the development process, let's talk about *how*.

Simply put: in each step of the development process, there's a security step, too.

Take it.

That might sound like a big undertaking, but really it's not. It's just a small change. You already have all of the right people in the right room having the right conversations; you just need them to consider security as well. The activities that are more involved (such as security testing) are handled by your security partner anyway, so the additional burden on your own developers is offloaded.

Many companies use a linear-sequential software development methodology, such as Waterfall. In this type of development methodology, the entire development project is approached as a whole, with each phase being completed across the entire system before the next phase begins. Here's how you'd build security into this type of methodology:

1. **During requirements gathering**, you discuss the problem that the system needs to solve. Simply expand the discussion to also consider your threat model. The requirements of the system dictate the features you'll need to develop. That determines which assets the system needs to access. These determine which attackers to consider and which attack surfaces to secure.

2. **During design**, you define the system architecture, determining which components to build and how they'll interact. Those inform how to implement Defense in Depth, a security approach that layers defenses in order to both minimize likelihood of breach and minimize damage resulting from a breach. (We'll explore this deeper in a moment.)

3. **During implementation**, you code the system. You know which areas of code are critical to security, and have those areas reviewed for security flaws specifically. You most likely aren't doing the security code review yourself anyway; your security partner is. So this important step isn't even a burden on your developers.

4. **During testing**, you evaluate system performance. In addition to functional testing, this is when you also do security testing. It happens in parallel with other testing efforts and is performed by your security partner. This frees your engineering resources to focus on other things. Vulnerabilities are discovered and reported to you so you can fix them. You'll invest effort in remediations, but as you learned in chapter 5, there's a way to manage that effort so it doesn't overwhelm you.

5. **During deployment**, you roll the solution out to customers and deal with the inevitable challenges that come with that. Now is when you also advise customers on configuration so they deploy your system securely. Whether this comes as documentation or hands-on

configuration assessment (or both), they're supplied by your security partner. Thus, the system is deployed securely without too much effort from you.

6. **During maintenance**, you're in the never-ending cycle of resolving bugs. Same idea with security. Through reassessments, your security evaluators help you continually find and fix security flaws. As a result, you keep your system secure over time, all without too much heavy lifting by you.

So, to summarize, your security efforts look like this:

Stage	Development Action	Security Action
Requirements	Determine business and user needs	Establish threat model
Design	Define architecture	Design Defense in Depth
Implementation	Write code	Audit code
Testing	Perform QA testing	Perform vulnerability assessment and remediations
Deployment	Commence customer rollout	Assess configuration
Maintenance	Resolve bugs	Perform reassessments

You can apply these same principles if you adhere to an iterative methodology instead, such as Agile, Scrum, Kanban, or Rapid Application Development. Iterative methodologies are where a large development project is broken down into smaller chunks. Development then cycles through requirements, design, implementation, testing, and deployment on each *feature* (rather than on the *entire project*, as you would in a linear-sequential development methodology). These features are often referred to as "user stories," which describes the feature from an end user's perspective. To build security into this type of development process, all of the same actions mentioned above occur, done for each feature (or "user story") as you cycle through them. Here's how:

ITERATIVE SOFTWARE DEVELOPMENT METHODOLOGIES

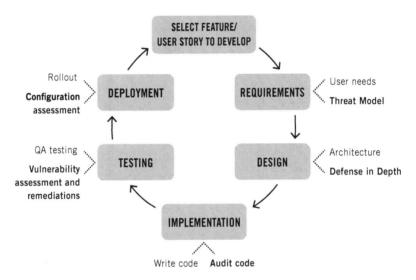

Whether you use a linear-sequential development process like Waterfall or an iterative one like Agile, you can—and must—build security in. If this guidance still doesn't address your unique development challenges, I'm only an email away: *ted@tedharrington.com*. Contact me and I'll point you in the right direction.

As one of our security analysts put it, "Think about security when you're doing things, not after you already did things."

ASSUME BREACH:
IMPLEMENT DEFENSE IN DEPTH

The harsh reality is that many apps will get hacked eventually.

Maybe it's because the system has vulnerabilities that the victim doesn't know about. Maybe it's because they fail to effectively fix vulnerabilities they *do* know about. Maybe it's because their third-party libraries have vulnerabilities, and they didn't realize that it's their job to mitigate. Who knows, somewhere in the supply chain there may be a zero-day vulnerability.

Whatever the reason, you should assume that your attackers are gunning for you, too. Once you accept this and weave it into everything you do, it positions you to thwart their efforts. You want to build layers of defenses. This minimizes the chances they'll get past your defense measures and also minimizes the chances they'll actually compromise your assets even if they do. As you build *the system*, always be thinking about how to build *security* into it.

You may be familiar with the Tower of London, the iconic castle known for its imposing presence on the river Thames. I was recently on a trip to London to deliver a keynote and found myself passing this iconic sight on a morning run. I stopped, noticing the least remarkable of features:

The moat.

Like many castles, the Tower of London has a wide, deep moat. It has a massive drawbridge. It has two concentric rings of perimeter walls. Within those walls are guards, trap doors, secret escape routes, and fortified compartments.

Together these demonstrate the principle of Defense in Depth: a security approach that layers defenses in order to both minimize *likelihood* of breach and minimize *damage* resulting from a breach.

Defense in Depth is a critical component of your security strategy. It helps you assume you've already been or soon will be breached. That helps you take action.

Too often, companies apply the wrong breach mindset. They simply try to keep attackers out, overlooking what happens if they get in. Instead, if you assume breach, you implement measures that make it both harder to break in and harder to extract your valuable assets. That's Defense in Depth. Attackers won't like it when you do this because it makes their job harder—which is precisely the point.

To do this effectively, ask this about each of your defenses: "What if they get past _____? How do I prevent further damage?"

Here are just a few ways to think about this in your app. (This gets a little technical, but I always want to be as specific as possible, especially when the advice is about tasks you can do in-house instead of outsourcing.)

- If you're filtering inputs to prevent XSS, make sure to filter inputs both before data enters a database and after it comes out, in case a developer inadvertently exposes a path that skips filtering on the input side.

- In cloud deployments, avoid leaving everything open after you get past the perimeter. Assume resources such as compute instances will be compromised and make sure everything can communicate with only the specific other resources that they need to.

- To minimize the window where a compromised user can cause damage, especially when accessing administrative interfaces or production servers, implement MFA.

- To further bolster the defenses you build into your app, add systems such as web application firewalls, intrusion prevention systems, and antivirus solutions (just be careful to avoid the trap of thinking that these alone will protect your app—they won't, at least not alone. Many people make that mistake).

This short list is not exhaustive; these are just a few examples for reference. There are many other ways to implement Defense in Depth. The point is simply this: assume you've already been breached and then implement layers of defenses accordingly.

It's often lamented that the defender has to be right every time, whereas the attacker has to be right only once. Defense in Depth flips that on its head. When you've properly implemented Defense in Depth, it gives you time and multiple mechanisms to catch an attacker and stop him in his tracks. The attacker has to get every step perfectly right in order to successfully bypass each defense without detection. At the same time, the defender needs to flag the attacker only once to stop him.

NO, SECURITY DOES NOT SLOW YOU DOWN

Many software companies tend to think that security slows down the development process. It's seen as important for sure but not as the most important thing *right now*. It's seen as something that can come later. It's seen as something that causes delays in hitting release milestones and overall makes lives harder for developers.

There's just one thing, though: it's not true. It's one of the biggest fallacies in all of computer science. *"Security slows me down!"* False.

I completely empathize with people who think this: there's intense pressure to meet deadlines. They're rushed to release the next version, and anything that can be postponed must be. Security is seen as one of those things.

But that makes your life harder, costs more, and is less effective. It's taking a short-term view on a long-term problem. When you delay security now, you accept massive slowdowns in the long run.

It's a lot easier than most people realize to build security into the development process. Did you notice how easily those security actions dovetail with your existing development actions? Building security into the development process simply capitalizes on existing engineering efforts. It requires some additional conversations and some consulting fees, but it doesn't inherently imperil deadlines. By contrast, do you know what *definitely does* imperil deadlines? Building a product whose flaws force a hard choice: release an insecure solution or start over.

Yikes. If "start over" isn't a gut punch, then I don't know what is.

Here's an example: we work with a company whose software facilitates online banking. When they hired us, they'd already been in the market for a little while and felt it was time to start digging deeper into security. After completing the initial security assessment, we discovered that the system was catastrophically flawed. The problems were so profound that as built, this system would never be strong enough to protect bank accounts. Attackers want your money! A system this flawed wouldn't be able to protect it.

Our recommendation: complete redesign. Rebuild the entire solution from scratch. Otherwise, they'll eventually be the cause of a disastrous breach where bank accounts get emptied.

That was a hard recommendation to make, and it was hard for them to hear. They'd invested several years and millions of dollars in development. If they'd engaged security during the design phase rather than several years later, they could have invested their time and money in developing something much more viable. Instead, they have a painful, slow road ahead.

My heart goes out to them. If only they'd had this book in their hands! If only someone had advised them to build security into the development process. Alas, that didn't happen, and as a result, here they are. But you don't have to be! Let's transform their misfortune into a positive outcome by helping you avoid the same fate. Reject the lie that security slows you down, because in reality, what *really* slows you down is postponing security. Delay is your silent killer. It's your carbon monoxide.

When you reject that lie, when you "build security in," you make small investments now that return big savings later. Like investing in your retirement accounts, consistent contributions over time deliver exponential payoffs down the road.

Build security into the development process, and you'll get better security that costs you less.

BIG IDEAS

Build security into the development process: it is more effective and less expensive than delaying security.

- You want to build security in: consider it throughout the development process. You do not want to bolt security on: consider it only after the solution is built.

- It's less expensive to build security in. You save on both consulting fees and on your own development effort.

- It's more effective to build security in. When you consider security in each stage of the development process, it delivers you a much more effective security model than if you do not.

- In order to build security in, there is a security action to take at each stage of the development process. This is true whether you use a linear-sequential or iterative development methodology.

- Assume you've already been breached, and then implement layers of defenses accordingly.

- Done right, security does not slow you down; in fact, it saves you headache and heartache in the long run.

For downloadable templates, team exercises, and real-world examples, go to *tedharrington.com/hackable*.

You've built a better, more secure product. You've found numerous ways to spend money and time more efficiently and more effectively. Now let's wrap it all up by answering one last question: how do you use security to *make* money, too?

CAUTION!

Security delivers a
competitive advantage.

You're about to learn how to use
it to earn trust and win sales.

**_However_, these only apply
if you do security right!**

If you implement the ideas
in this book, the following
chapter applies to you.

If you do not implement the
ideas in this book, the following
chapter does not apply to you.

CHAPTER 10

WIN SALES

LIE
Security is a tax.

TRUTH
Security is an investment.

atching a crab sucks.

It happens in rowing, a brutal sport that is mostly all pain and no fun. When your team is in sync, the boat is flying on the top of the water, and you're winning—it's pretty magical. But sometimes, you "catch a crab." A stroke lands at a bad angle, causing the water to rip the oar out of your hands. The handle rams your chest, slamming you backward into the teammate behind you. Everyone on the boat collides. No longer rowing, the oars become brakes. The boat screeches to a halt. You lose the race every time.

It's enormously demoralizing.

That's how most software companies experience the dreaded part of the sales process: when your customer wants to talk about security. The team is in sync, working at an all-out effort, flying toward the finish line...and then security slams you in the chest. It knocks you into your teammates. Everyone falls out of sync and stops moving forward. Competitors beat you to the finish. The team is totally demoralized.

Sound familiar?

If so, you're not alone. Security has become an essential requirement in most buying processes. Your ability to both (a) be secure and (b) prove it to your customer are absolutely critical if you want to win sales. Most people don't know how to do either part right. But because you've read this book, you know how to do the first part right. All that remains is to get the second part right, too. Then you'll never catch a crab again.

When you do security right, it gives you a competitive edge that helps you win sales.

SECURITY IS A DIFFERENTIATOR

"Every bit of security adds value to your customers," a CTO told me. Some security is what he calls "table stakes": the basics that everyone must do. Everything else—the things that separate those who do security right from those who don't—are differentiators. As he explains, "Being clear about our security strategy helps the buying conversations with our customers. They see it as a differentiator."

Here's why I agree with him:

- Most companies don't understand security, let alone how to do it right. Now you do.

- Most companies don't understand their attackers and don't have a threat model. Now you do.

- Most companies invest too little, too infrequently, with too little collaboration, using the wrong methods focused only on the issues of too little significance. You'll be doing the opposite of each.

- *Most companies are not secure. You will be.*

Consider how powerful that contrast is. It's incredibly differentiating.

Your customer is just as worried about security as you are. They're excited to work with companies like yours, who address these concerns.

EARN TRUST

To use security to drive sales, you need to get your customer to trust you first. If they do, they buy faster. If they don't, they hit the brakes and proceed with caution.

The opposite of trust is fear. You introduce fear when you make hollow promises, misleading claims, and fail to back claims up.

Hollow promises are when words don't line up with actions. For example, every breach notification letter always seems to include the phrase "We take your security seriously." But do they? After all, they were compromised. Is that because they cut corners, skipping the things you learned to do in this book?

Misleading claims are when someone inappropriately tries to imply a broader truth about a specific fact. For example, when people claim "bank-level security," they're trying to suggest that because they use the same encryption that banks use, they must be as secure as a bank. That's not necessarily true. It also misrepresents how attackers operate: they typically don't try to break encryption. They attack softer targets.

Failing to back up claims is when insufficient evidence is provided to support security claims. For example, companies commonly say that their app is "highly secure" but don't explain what that means or how to verify it.

Don't do those things.

They imply that you don't know what you're doing. That builds fear. You've read this book, so by now, you actually *do* know what you're doing. But if you make hollow promises, misleading claims, and fail to back up claims, you lump yourself in with all of the other chumps who don't know how to do security right.

You want to avoid that. You want to make sure that your customers know that you're different...because you *are* different.

So instead of building *fear*, build *trust*. You do this by being transparent. It's pretty simple, so let's not overcomplicate it:

1. **Tell 'em** your security philosophy.

2. **Tell 'em** what you did, how you did it, what you found, and how you'll fix it.

3. **Tell 'em** how to verify what you're saying.

Simple as that. Security is not a trick. There's no need to mislead or make unsupported claims. Just be frank. Be straightforward about what testing you're doing, why, and how to verify it.

When you ask questions of other people, you want them to give you the straight truth. That's exactly what your customers want from you, too.

Apply these principles to each of the following tactics, and you'll be on the fast track to earning trust.

Trust leads to sales.

TACTIC #1:
USE YOUR SECURITY ASSESSMENT REPORT

Any good security assessment delivers a report. It's a powerful tool. Share it with your customers. It helps them understand what you're doing. They want that insight.

You can use a summary of this report in many situations:

- **Send** when prospecting new accounts.

- **Send** before sales calls.

- **Review** during sales calls.

- **Send** on a regular cadence (such as quarterly) to demonstrate your ongoing commitment to security.

- **Post** to your website for download (which I'll explain more in tactic #5).

From *Fortune* 5 enterprises to funded startups (and everyone in between), companies of all sizes do these things to successfully support their sales processes. You can, too.

In most cases, the report itself is too sensitive to share: it contains attack details on how to exploit your system and usually reveals proprietary information about how your system works. I'd advise against sharing that version. Instead, what you (probably) want to send is an executive summary. That report version redacts out attack details and proprietary system info, while still helping your customer verify your security claims, approach, and posture. (If your security assessments don't result in this deliverable, take a hard look at why not. You may be investing in the wrong approach or even the wrong partner.)

A word of caution, though: not all reports are created equal. Some are little more than bloated outputs from automated tools. Instead, make sure your report discusses scope, methodology, threat model, vulnerabilities found, severity ratings, and recommended fixes. These elements of course help you get better, but they're also what makes the report a compelling sales tool. Don't live without them.

TACTIC #2: USE YOUR SECURITY CONSULTANTS IN SALES MEETINGS

When your customer brings up security concerns during the sales process, consider involving your security partner. Have them meet with your customer. You walk away with either the concerns resolved or clear direction on how to resolve them. You earn your customer's confidence that you *truly* understand their concerns and can address them. Better yet, you also make your own life easier by deputizing your security partner to handle this critical element. Win-win.

When it comes to their security concerns, your customers are looking for the candid truth. They want objective facts. They want insight to help make a decision. However, they may think that you're biased in this conversation. They know that you want the sale. They may assume that would influence what you tell (or don't tell) them. Your security consultant resolves this scenario. Security consultants should be independent: that means they wouldn't say anything untrue or mislead your customer; they'll just stick to the facts.[29] Your customer wants that. Having an objective voice in the security conversation assures that they're getting the straight truth. It helps your customer make an informed decision. The faster they can make an informed decision, the faster both you and your customer can move forward in your business relationship. The faster you can close the sale.

Another benefit is that the authority of your security consultant transfers to you. Your developers, and even your internal security team, don't spend every waking moment breaking systems. But ethical hackers do. Your security partner studies the adversary every day. They know how attackers think and how they operate. They know how to find security vulnerabilities that matter. They know how to build secure products. Your customer likes all of this. It means that they can get their questions answered effectively, with authority. It even means your customer might learn something in the process (and everyone loves free consulting!). By bringing your security consultants into a meeting directly with your customer, you deliver value by addressing their concerns. In the process, *you* look good.

---

29 Make sure your partner does indeed deliver these things. If not, this tactic won't work.

Finally, your security consultants create order out of chaos. There are uncertainties about the security of your application. There are uncertainties about what matters to your customer. There are uncertainties about the methods used by your attackers. Security consultants understand all of these things.

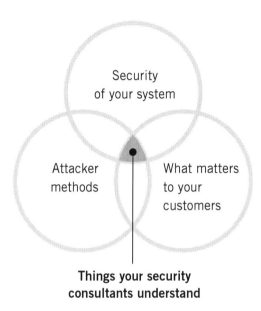

Things your security consultants understand

The VP of engineering from a client recently called me in a panic. Her customer had just told her no. They would not sign a contract because, as they told her, "Your architecture violates our security model. Unless you redesign it, we won't accept it."

Her company had been doing security right. They had the right goal, were investing appropriately in it, and were well on their way to security excellence. Yet, security nevertheless became a blocker to sales. The engineering effort to redesign the system would be so massive that it was not a real possibility; that meant that this rejection was essentially permanent.

To remedy this, she invited us to a meeting with her and her customer. It turns out that her customer was worried about the security ramifications of cloud-based workflows. Or at least, that was the *stated* concern. Through probing questions, we learned that they were actually concerned about migrating to a new security model: from on-premises to cloud. It wasn't about *cloud*; it was about *change*. They weren't sure how to handle this change.

Fortunately, we deeply understood this scenario from having helped many other companies through the same thing. Although we want our customers to succeed, we never violate our independence. We remained neutral, stuck to the facts, and explained things in objective terms. We didn't even recommend that they buy this solution; we simply answered their security questions. We asked our own questions, too, in order to ensure we understood the underlying concerns. We addressed those as well. Once we understood the buyer's concerns and how they'd deploy the system, we walked them through the system architecture, helping them understand the security implications. It turns out that it actually *supported* the existing security paradigm and did not *violate* it (which we helped explain).

As a result, the meeting went smoothly. Barely forty-five minutes later, the buyer sat back in his chair and said warmly, "Well, that settles it. This actually *does* work for us. Let's get procurement involved."

Our client was ecstatic. Security had been a hurdle. Now it no longer was. They removed security as a blocker to sales.

You can, too.

TACTIC #3:
MAKE SECURITY QUESTIONNAIRES POP

Security questionnaires are an attempt by your customer to document your security posture, policies, and controls. The purpose is to understand the risk they'd be accepting if they use your system. However, they're also a great sales and marketing opportunity for *you* if you do them right.

Companies get in their own way when they try to cut corners, ignore elements, or minimize the importance of these documents. Don't do that. I assure you, these questionnaires matter to your customer. If it matters to them, it matters to you. Instead, make these documents work *for* you. If you do, they support your sales effort.

Here's how to make them pop:

- **Answer every question**. Some questions might not apply to you. Don't skip them! Instead, explain why the question doesn't apply. Brushing it off with just "N/A: not applicable" fails to address your customer's concerns. That only does one thing: forces them to invest more time and ask more questions. They're asking because they need to understand, so help them understand! By skipping questions, you make your customer's life harder, which is not exactly the path to great relationships. But by answering every question, including explaining why a given question doesn't apply, you make your customer's life easier.

- **Be concise**. Stick to the facts. Answer in the context of the question being asked. Give enough information to ensure your customer has the answer, but avoid going on tangents. Your customer reviews a lot of these. They want just the facts. They can tell when they're being fed rubbish. Get to the point fast.

- **Be clear**. Although you want to be concise, also be sure to explain sufficiently. Give details. Make it easy to understand what you're doing and how that relates to the question at hand. Even if you lack a security feature that is specifically being asked about, that's OK. Say that. You'd be surprised how often your customers will be fine with that. Just be clear.

- **Clarify**. Questions are often confusing and poorly phrased. Sometimes they use acronyms or jargon that make sense to your customer but are indecipherable to you. Don't ignore these or answer them wrong. Instead, simply ask your customer to clarify. Both of you want the question to be answered appropriately, so strive for clarity.

- **Understand your audience**. Sometimes you're dealing with seasoned security pros, sometimes with novices. Some need the basics explained; others want you to skip the basics and focus on the complexities. You need to know who is reading the questionnaire responses, what their security proficiency is, and what their expectations are. Craft your responses accordingly.

This requires you to invest effort up front in building rapport, but if you do, it increases the probability that your responses resonate.

If you do these things, it smooths the path to acceptance. You make your customer's life easier. You remove one more brick in the wall between you and the sale.

Now, this might feel like a lot. If you get many of these questionnaires, the idea of thoroughly answering every question on all of them might seem overwhelming. If so, there is another way: hand them to your security consultant.

Your security partner eliminates this hassle for you. This also ensures that the questionnaires are done right. It puts your security expert in direct dialogue with your customer, which fosters trust faster. This will cost you in fees, and not all security assessors can do this effectively. However, those tradeoffs may be worth it to save time and make sure they're done right.

To illustrate, consider what happened when a major enterprise's CISO quit. Members of his staff were left scrambling to deal with the security questionnaires coming across his now-vacant desk. The burden of these questionnaires fell to the VP of engineering. He was overwhelmed by this new duty. We'd been doing security assessments of their application suite for some time, so he asked us to handle the questionnaires. We understood the technical details of their apps and we understood the questions in the forms, so it was a no-brainer for us to help in this way.

As a result, the VP no longer had to worry about the questionnaires. He was able to focus on his core duties. Their customers were satisfied with the responses we submitted.

This enterprise saw no hiccups related to the questionnaires, despite the very disruptive departure of the security leader in charge of them.

Whether you do them yourself or enlist your security partner, the point is the same: capitalize on the opportunity. Security questionnaires are a chance to make your customer's life easier while building trust faster. Take it.

TACTIC #4: ALIGN YOUR REMEDIATION PLAN TO YOUR DEVELOPMENT ROADMAP

Security vulnerabilities will pretty much always exist; it's simply the nature of software development. There's no such thing as a "clean bill of health," the mistaken notion that an application has no vulnerabilities. The question is not whether vulnerabilities *exist*. Instead, the question is whether you've *found* them and whether you've *fixed* them. When you learned about vulnerability severity in chapter 5, you learned how to prioritize remediations and why. Empower your customers with this information, too. Show them your plan for what you'll fix and when you'll fix it. Help them understand that excellence is a journey. It doesn't happen instantly. This smooths the path to acceptance, even despite the existence of security vulnerabilities.

The best way to do this is to align your remediation plan to your development roadmap. Literally tell your customer when you'll fix each vulnerability. Some security vulnerabilities you need to fix immediately; others you can get to over time.

Here's an example of how:

When ↓ Timeframe	What ↓ Development action	Reference the vulnerabilities listed in your report ↓ Remediation
Q2	Implement single sign-on (SSO)	Resolve ISE-001-8789 Resolve ISE-001-8790 Resolve ISE-001-8791 Resolve ISE-001-8792
Q3	Improve user data encryption	Resolve ISE-001-8793 Resolve ISE-001-8794 Resolve ISE-001-8795

Your customers want to use software that is secure. For that reason, you may worry that the presence of security vulnerabilities would prevent them from moving forward with you. But the irony is that by showing your vulnerabilities, you actually *reassure* your customer. It calms them to see that you have a plan. It's comforting for them to see that you find your vulnerabilities and you fix them. They can see how rigorous your security approach is. They can make informed decisions about the risk they are accepting.

Now, this doesn't necessarily mean they'll be OK moving forward before you fix the vulnerabilities. But it definitely *does* mean that you've removed the lingering question in the back of their mind: "What are you hiding?" That unspoken question prevents trust. Because you're not hiding anything, you squash that concern. This makes everyone feel better, and the discussions can then focus on what problems *actually* exist, rather than wondering what *might* exist. They don't want the "monster to jump up and bite them in the butt," and you're showing them exactly what the monster might look like. They realize there's a plan to deal with it.

This gives you breathing room. If all you showed your customer was an unranked list of vulnerabilities, they'd probably want them all fixed immediately. By describing severity and outlining your plan to remediate the most urgent issues now and the lesser urgent items over time, you earn yourself the time to fix the vulnerabilities. You obviously can't defer remediations for too long, but you avoid having to stop all other development efforts in order to solely focus on remediations. This both satisfies your customer and makes your life better, all while keeping development marching forward.

By aligning your remediation plan to your development roadmap, you shine in stark contrast to your competition. Your competitors will suggest that they have no vulnerabilities. They'll try to claim that they have a "clean bill of health," that they are "highly secure," and that everything is just fantastic. By now, we all know that's not true. Vulnerabilities exist. Use that to your advantage. Simply communicate to your customers what's going on, and you'll build trust through transparency. They'll appreciate you for it.

TACTIC #5:
BUILD A SECURITY PAGE ON YOUR WEBSITE

Many companies talk about security on their website. You should, too. While writing this book, I did a little investigation, reviewing two hundred marketing websites of prominent, enterprise-class applications. I was looking to see whether they talk about security, and if they do, what they say. More than 45 percent of them talk about security in some form or another, with more than two-thirds of those having an entire page dedicated to it. This shows that other software companies also recognize the demand for security. You need to address it, too.

However, almost all of them do it wrong. If you do it right, that creates enormous opportunity for you. Of all the sites examined in my study, less than 4 percent of them talk about the level of rigor you've learned in this book.

Less than 4 percent do it right! More than 96 percent do it wrong! Think about that for a moment.

(a) Customers demand security. It's a powerful differentiator.

(b) Almost no one capitalizes on it.

A + B = opportunity!

So capture the benefit of your investment by talking about security right. Build a web page that is specific to security. It could be a page on your existing marketing site or a new standalone site; it works either way. Discuss your security in terms that your customer cares about. Help them understand what's in it for them. This is not about you; it's about them. Make it super clear what you're doing, and explain why they should care.

Describe things in simple, clear, honest, straightforward language. Don't overcomplicate it. Don't overload it with jargon. Don't fluff it up with marketing-speak. Just be direct. This will strongly differentiate from the nonsense out in the marketplace.

The more thorough and transparent you are, the more powerfully differentiating it is. When your competitors make hollow, misleading claims without backing them up, your transparency shines in sharp contrast. It strongly resonates with your customers. It speaks to the deep-seated fears they have about their security and about your security.

Here's how:

1. **State your security mission**: For example, that might be something like "Our mission is to be known as..." and then describe what you're trying to achieve with security. Discuss it in the context of your overall company mission. Use language that makes your customer the center of the claim.

2. **Describe your internal security team (if you have one)**: "In pursuit of this mission, we have built a well-rounded internal security department, specializing in..." and then outline the core capabilities of your internal team. Describe how those capabilities support that mission. Remember, frame each of these statements around *your customer*. Help them understand what's in it for them. In this case, that would mean describing how the capabilities of the internal team directly impact the outcome your customer is looking for. (If you don't have an internal security team, you can skip this part.)

3. **Back up any claims you make**: "You can read more about how we do that here..." and link to where the reader can read or download any documentation supporting your claims.

4. **Describe your approach to security testing**: This portion is critical. While most of your competitors barely

scratch the surface with their testing, you go deep. Don't miss the opportunity to differentiate! It's yours for the taking! Explain how your approach is different and why it's beneficial to your customer. For example, you might say, "We engage in quarterly, manual, white-box security assessments with..." (or whatever methodology and cadence you pursue) and then command the authority of your security partner by naming them and including a link to their website. Here's where you really need to show them how thorough your approach to security is so it contrasts with the hollow, misleading, unbacked-up claims that everyone else makes.

5. **Provide reports so your customers can verify**: "Read a summary of our most recent security assessment report..." and include a method to download, access, or request it. And very importantly, when someone requests it, *actually share it!* I know a company that only responds to those requests with salespeople who refuse to send a report. That makes me doubt that any reports even exist. You can require customers to meet with you first in order to share it if that makes you feel more comfortable. But you need to share it. Otherwise, they'll wonder: what are you hiding? (As you can see, behavior like that builds fear, not trust.)

6. **Describe security functionality in your app**: "We've built a robust set of security features that protects your most valuable assets, including..." and then outline each security feature in simple language, how it works, and

how your customer can verify that it's a good feature. Again, make it clear why your customer should care and how this helps them. It's about them, not about you.[30]

7. **Describe other security initiatives that demonstrate your security mission, and back them up, too:** "We work closely with the security research community; researchers can submit vulnerabilities here..." and include a link or email address where researchers can submit. Describe any other notable initiatives here, too.

8. **Call back to your mission, tie it to your ethos, and make it easy to contact you about security questions:** "We are always looking to get better, so contact us to discuss any security questions at..." and insert your security-specific email address. You need a dedicated way to contact you about security. It needs to be easy to find. And you need to respond to it.

This might feel like a lot. But you know what? It's what your customers are looking for. So give it to them!

You don't need to follow this script verbatim, but you do need to make it clear what you're doing, why it should matter to your customer, and how they can verify what you claim. You need to highlight that what you're doing is more thorough than

---

30 If you want to better understand how to do this, read my friend Bruce Turkel's legendary book *All About Them*. You'll thank me later. Bruce Turkel, *All About Them: Grow Your Business by Focusing on Others* (Boston: Da Capo Lifelong Books, 2016).

what most companies do, and you need to do so with authenticity and transparency.

The final recommendation here is about navigation. Don't bury the link to your security page in the website footer. That's where most people hide their security page (when they have one at all). I do use that word intentionally because that's what it looks like—it looks like they're *hiding* it, not *promoting* it. Instead, include the security page in the navigation at the top of your website. Almost no one does this. When you do, it will absolutely scream to your customers, "Security matters to us!" They'll like that.

SECURITY THROUGH OBSCURITY: PLEASE DON'T!

Let's pause for a quick vibe check. You may worry that revealing information helps your attackers. If so, you're getting caught in the lie known as "security through obscurity," a fallacy that relies on secrecy as the primary defense mechanism.

Secrecy is a good thing. You should add it to your security efforts where you can. But secrecy alone should not be what your security model depends on. In fact, you need to assume that all secrets are known.

Imagine that you have a duffel bag full of cash. You want to hide your small fortune, so you go deep into the woods and bury it. You are the only person who knows where. Pretty secure, right?

Now imagine that someone saw you digging this random hole deep in the woods. She got curious. The only thing between that person and your cash is some overturned dirt. Would you still feel as confident now that the secret is gone? Probably not.

Secrecy is an additional layer that you can (and should!) add to your defense plan, but it shouldn't be the primary element. Instead, adhere to Kerckchoff's principle, which says that a system should be secure even if everything about the system (except the key) is public knowledge. If you can do that successfully, then you're clear to implement the kind of transparency outlined in this chapter. You can communicate your security approach in ways that help your customers without ceding the advantage to your attackers.

A NOTE OF CAUTION

Security delivers a competitive advantage. It helps you with marketing. It helps you close sales!

However...

This *only* works if you do security right.

Step one: secure your app.

Step two: prove it.

That order of operations is irreversible. You can't do it the other way around. You can't try to prove that your app is secure if you didn't secure it in the first place. Sounds obvious, but you'd be shocked how often people try to do exactly that. This happens either because people don't *know* how to do security right, don't *want* to do security right, or simply want to take a *shortcut* to the marketing benefit. Much of what's wrong with security today results from people trying to skip the "security" part. It simply doesn't work that way.

If you cut corners, look only for the basic issues, invest poorly, apply too little effort, limit information, pursue the wrong testing types, rely only on automated scans alone, skip the hard stuff, fail to implement remediations, skip your threat model, or fail to adapt to change, you simply *cannot* capitalize on the many marketing and sales benefits that security delivers. You *must* implement the ideas in this book in order to take advantage.

Good security delivers good marketing. Not the other way around.

A FINAL CASE STUDY: USING SECURITY TO WIN SALES

Easy to exploit, and delivers catastrophic compromise.

That's pretty much the last thing you want. It's what happened when one of our customers accidentally introduced a vulnerability that allowed authentication bypass. This enabled an attacker to access resources without verifying identity. In this case, it meant that anyone—literally anyone in the world—could access the app's most valuable assets without any sort of login. It was a critical vulnerability, to say the least.

Here's the unexpected part: they used it to win sales.

They didn't *hide* the flaw; they *highlighted* it. Once they fixed the issue, they talked about it to all of their customers. It became part of their narrative. However, it wasn't really about the flaw itself; it was about their *approach*. They found (and fixed) this critical security vulnerability because they did security right— by following every element of the method you've learned in this book. Without the appropriate approach, they wouldn't have been able to find this issue, let alone fix it. They used this vulnerability—and the rigorous process that enabled them to find and fix it—as a means to demonstrate their journey to security excellence. They proved that they knew how to do security right.

They proved that they've built a better, more secure product. They proved that they are worthy of trust.

This resonated—not *despite* the flaw but *because* of it. Buyers liked how authentic and transparent this company was being. They could understand this company's security philosophy. They could see firsthand how aggressively this company hunts down and eradicates vulnerabilities. They could see that this company wasn't just paying lip service to security; they were going after it hard.

As a result, they earned customers. Tons of them.

Imagine that. A security vulnerability is what *drove* sales, rather than *preventing* sales. Therein lies the beauty of security done right. You build better, more secure software, and then people want to pay you for it.

Do these things.

Go win.

BIG IDEAS

When you do security right, it gives you a competitive edge that helps you win sales.

- Security is a differentiator.

- Earn trust; don't build fear. You build fear by making hollow promises, misleading claims, and failing to back up claims. You build trust by being transparent instead.

- Use your security assessment report as marketing collateral.

- Use your security assessor in sales meetings.

- Make security questionnaires pop.

- Align your remediation plan to your development roadmap.

- Build a security-specific website or web page.

- Transparency is OK; don't get trapped by security through obscurity.

- Step one is secure your app. Step two is prove it. You can't do it the other way around.

For downloadable templates, team exercises, and real-world examples, go to *tedharrington.com/hackable*.

You did it! You've learned the method: how to think, how to break, how to fix, and how to convert all of that into sales! Now go take action.

GO WIN

That bull nearly gored me to death.

Given such a narrow escape, you'd probably expect me to get the hell out of there. I did not. Instead, I hopped back down from the fence and started chasing after the bulls. I wanted to know where they go! Eventually, I came to a dead end at the grand old building where the bullfights take place. A rational person would have called it quits there, but I was overwhelmed with curiosity. Were the bulls inside? Was the event over? What happens next? At that moment, the tall, ornately carved doors of the building were closing. I slipped in just before they did. Inside, I found myself standing in the center of the bullring itself, along with a few other curious runners like me. Standing there in the gritty sand felt like being a Roman gladiator. It was a pretty epic moment.

Then I noticed something peculiar: the stands around me were full of spectators. Before I could figure out why, the situation got real: a bull was released into the ring. An angry, dangerous, fast bull. There was no way out.

It was an intense moment. Time slowed down. Hair stood on end. Heart hammered in my chest.

I was in a very serious situation and I had no choice but to deal with it. The bull—already aggressive by nature and now further agitated in this confined space surrounded by cheering crowds—started rushing those of us in the ring with him. Everyone wanted to touch the bull because apparently, that's good luck. But all this did was piss off the bull further. People got rammed, tossed, dirty, and bloodied. It was absolute mayhem. I had a close call of my own, when just as I was considering giving the bull a kick in the butt, he turned. He looked me square in the eyes, clearly contemplating whether to charge me...before someone else caught his attention.

Eventually, some handlers came out and wrangled the bull back into his pen. The doors of the bullring opened to let us out. In an adrenaline-infused daze, an unexpected, hilarious thought slapped me in the face:

I can do it better next time.

That's where you are right now in your security mission. Feet planted squarely in the gritty sand of the bullring, ready to master the situation before you. Ready to face incoming threats. Ready to do better.

You can do this. I know you can. *You* know you can.

Application security is hard. It's complex, chaotic, and may not even be your entire job.

But now you know what to do.

It all boils down to a few simple ideas: to do application security right, stop doing it wrong. Relentlessly pursue security excellence. Spend money better, and spend time better, too. Find your security vulnerabilities so you can fix them. Build better, more secure products. Prove it to your customers. As a result, get the benefits that are delivered when security is done right—not just the technical benefits of a more secure product but the business benefits, too. Gain a competitive edge. Earn trust. Win sales.

Now that you've read this book, you have all the tools. You know how to think, how to execute, and how to win. You've spotted the lies and replaced them with truths. You have the method. It's time for action!

As you step out into the bullring, remember a few keys to your success:

1. APPROACH MATTERS

Start with the right mindset and the right partner. Apply the right methodology to the right type of testing. Taken together, these ideas ensure that you're pointing the arrow directly at the center of the bull's-eye you're trying to hit.

2. ATTACK IT TO IMPROVE IT

Hack your system, then fix it, then hack it again. Go beyond the fundamentals and execute the advanced tactics in order to find your most critical (and unexpected) security vulnerabilities— because your attackers are going to do that, too. That's how you eradicate that nagging feeling of "I don't know what I don't know." Make sure you establish your threat model so you can understand the battle you're in (and win it).

3. SAVE MONEY, MAKE MONEY

Security isn't a *tax*; it's an *investment*. Make sure you spend wisely—you can't go cheap, but you don't need to spend endlessly either. When you do security right, it's more effective and less expensive. You can save costs and reduce effort simply by building security into the development process. Same thing happens when you hit the right reassessment cadence, too. Better yet, security done right helps you earn trust and win sales. So security will make you money, too!

SECURITY IS A TEAM SPORT

You can execute some security actions with in-house experts, whereas other actions you need an external partner to do. Some actions you do together. Here's a quick recap:

Action	Who Does It
Think	
Constantly seek improvement. Think like an attacker.	Both your in-house resources and your external partner need to adopt these mindsets.
Hack	
Share information and transfer knowledge.	This goes both ways: in-house teams share information to make external experts more efficient with testing. External experts transfer knowledge to make in-house teams better.

Action	Who Does It
Hack (*continued*)	
Analyze system design, run scanners, look for common vulnerabilities, abuse functionality, chain exploits, seek unknown unknowns.	External partner.
Remediate	
Assign vulnerability severity.	External partner.
Prioritize remediations by severity.	Collaboration between in-house teams and your external partner.
Remediate vulnerabilities.	In-house.
Verify remediations.	External partner.
Hack Again	
Analyze system design, run scanners, look for common vulnerabilities, abuse functionality, chain exploits, seek unknown unknowns.	External partner.
Invest	
Determine appropriate budget.	Collaboration between in-house teams and your external partner, although ultimately, this call is made in-house.
Threat Modeling	
Determine assets to protect, adversaries to thwart, and attack surface to defend.	Collaboration between in-house teams and your external partner.

Action	Who Does It
Build Security In	
Implement appropriate security step at each stage of development.	In-house, with guidance from partner as needed.
Assume breach, and apply Defense in Depth.	In-house, with guidance from partner as needed.
Win Sales	
Build security page.	In-house, with guidance on talking points from your partner.
Use assessment report in sales process.	In-house.
Use security partner in sales process.	In-house team brings external partner into meetings.
Respond to security questionnaires.	In-house with guidance from partner or hand off to partner entirely.
Align remediation plan to development roadmap.	In-house, with guidance from external expert as needed.

IT GOES BEYOND THIS BOOK

My commitment to you does not end here. If you need further guidance on any of these ideas, contact me at *ted@tedharrington. com*. That's my personal email, and I *will* respond. It would be my honor to help you with any of this. When you succeed, I succeed. So don't hesitate to ask.

You may need additional resources: you can download many helpful items, including threat model templates, team exercises, security research examples, and more at *tedharrington.com/hackable*.

GET STARTED!

So get going. Right now.

You have all the tools. Go use them. Your journey doesn't end here. In fact, it's only just begun.

This isn't about your company. It isn't even about you. It's about the many people who rely on you—some wittingly, most unwittingly. They suffer if you don't do your job at the extreme utmost of your ability. People get fired, careers get ruined, companies go out of business.

But you can be their hero.

You can prevent these bad outcomes. You can achieve great outcomes instead. You can make your company prosper. You can make *yourself* prosper. When you take action on what you learned in this book, you serve everyone. You make your mark.

So now I pass the baton to you.

Go implement these ideas. Talk about them with your boss, peers, direct reports, friends, family, and industry community. If you're not sure where to start or feel overwhelmed, just pick a single idea and start there. Share this book with others who would benefit from it. Use me as a resource: email me, connect with me on LinkedIn, or come meet me after a keynote. I'll happily teach you whatever I can.

Drive for a better tomorrow. Build better, more secure products. Gain the competitive edge that security delivers. Achieve security excellence.

Go kick that bull's ass.

You got this.

PSST...

Did you notice the Easter egg code
embedded in the back cover design?

Do you want to learn how to
decipher the message?

65 47 78 74 63 6d 38 67 63
47 31 76 61 53 42 6c 49 47 78
6c 5a 32 39 70 64 67 6f 3d

Go to *tedharrington.com/hackable*
for a step-by-step walk-through.

#hackable

ACKNOWLEDGMENTS

Gratitude.

My heart is absolutely bursting with it.

Security truly is a team sport, and this book would not be possible without so many amazing, selfless, dedicated, intelligent people contributing to it. My name may be on the cover, but it shouldn't be alone. This book is better because of all of you.

My Scribe fam, in you I found not just other authors going through a shared experience: I found lifelong friends. Ron Thurston, Hussein Al-Baiaty, Sabreet Kang Rajeev, Colleen Healy, Dr. Kate Price, Craig Perkins, Lindsay Shoop, Rich Ezekiel, Joette Orman, Kelly Battaglia, and Glen Robison: you've made an indelible mark on my life. You advised me in my darkest moments and celebrated my brightest moments. They say that writing is a lonely journey, but with you all, it was exactly the opposite. You made this book better. You made me better.

Steve Bono, your friendship has quite literally changed my life. The things we're doing together in building ISE have been some of the most fulfilling experiences of my life. So much of this book is the result of this mission we are on together. Thank you for your brotherhood, mentorship, and always challenging me to be better.

Shea Polansky, your thumbprints are all over the best parts of this book. The care you put into helping me get the technical details right ensured that this book will help other people. I learned so much from you in the process. You made this book better. You made me better.

Kevin Thomas, you are a master at helping me shape ideas. You challenged me to tighten up the weak parts and strengthen the strong parts. You helped me spread the word about the book so we could impact as many lives as possible. You made this book better. You made me better.

Matt Stamper, you have been such an incredible friend, mentor, and guide for so many years. As a beta reader, you pushed me to sharpen the content and better serve the reader. You made this book better. You made me better.

Sam Levin, your ability to get to the essence of an idea, and communicate it with authenticity, is a trait I admire and aspire to. Over the months of discussing ideas with you, you honed my understanding of them. You made this book better. You made me better.

Lauren Quinn, where would I be without you?! Writing this book required so much coordination with so many people, amid intensely challenging logistical constraints. You solved all of that. By doing so, you enabled me to focus on improving the content so I could serve my readers. I could always rest easy knowing that you've got things handled. You made this book better. You made me better.

Thank you to the many ISE people who contributed time, energy, love, and wisdom to this monumental undertaking. David Petty, your beta edits and collaboration on metaphors were incredibly impactful. Adrian Bednarek, you provided endless stories and insightful wisdom. Luke Phillips, you helped me quantify trends and insights so I had powerful data to reference. Josh Meyer, you helped me describe exploit scenarios simply and clearly. Shaun Mirani, you helped me get definitions razor-sharp at times where precision really mattered. Shane Lester, you helped me describe nuanced and elegant attack scenarios simply and clearly. Paul Yun, you sharpened my organization of what application security includes. Brendan Ortiz, Ali Esparza, Omer Farooq, and Christopher Campbell, you all helped me understand the journey from student to computer scientist to ethical hacker and why the world has so few people with this critically needed skillset. Ronnie Rast, you helped me identify the key sound bites so we can easily share the ideas in this book. Eli Mezei, you've been a brother to me, and the ways you've helped develop not just my security skills but also my leadership skills have directly impacted the shape of this book. Rick Ramgattie, your work distinguishing the many confusing terms in security directly impacted elements of this book. All of you made this book better. All of you made me better.

To the many people in the security community who helped in so many different ways, thank you. Gary Hayslip, your friendship, mentorship, and advice on writing helped get this project off the ground. Eric Diehl, your relentless encouragement that I get this book out in the world had a real impact on me actually getting it done. Ben Stanbury, you've been a tremendous friend and sounding board about so many of the ideas in this book and in life in general. David Scott, you've given me so many ideas and advice over the years, not the least of which helped me narrow in on the book title. Darran Rolls, your advice on the book idea and its resonance with the audience helped shape this book into what it is today. Justin Handville, you helped me clarify the relationship between security and trust. All of you made this book better. All of you made me better.

To the many CEOs, CTOs, CIOs, CISOs, VPs, PMs, and other leaders who met with me during the writing process, thank you for helping me ensure I truly understand the problems you face. Thanks to you, this book is able to help people. Chuck Parker, Tim Claman, Joel Sloss, Adrian Graham, Art Cuyugan, Jason Gish, Jeremy Smith, Paige Adams, Carlos Pero, and Todd Prives: my gratitude is profound for you as humans as well as for your input. Thank you. All of you made this book better. All of you made me better.

Thank you to the 7CTOs community for your input. Krijn van der Raadt, Scott Brenton, Godfrey Duke, Travis Fawcett, Jeff Cours, Pete Hanlon, and Igor Mameshin: you all gave me profound insights into the struggles of the modern CTO so I could make sure this book addresses them squarely. Thank you Etienne de Bruin for building that community so I could tap these experts for their perspective. All of you made this book better. All of you made me better.

To my author friends who gave me so much advice and wisdom: it's on the shoulders of you giants that I stand. Bruce Turkel, this entire book is written to be all about them. Stephen Shapiro, your kindness and generosity is injected into this book. You made me and this book better.

Profound appreciation goes to my squad at Lioncrest Publishing. Tucker Max, JT McCormick, Rikki Jump, Hal Clifford, Emily Gindlesparger, Tiffany Fletcher, Erica Hoffman, Rachael Brandenburg, Jane Borden, Cristy Bertini, Lisa Caskey, Joyce Li, and the many others I never even saw toiling behind the scenes: you made this experience an incredible one. You helped me write the best book I could right now.

To my LinkedIn followers: you shaped this book more than you know. I posted about the book almost every day of the writing process, and you helped improve ideas and understand what resonated (and what didn't).

Mom and Dad, thank you for your relentless support and tireless interest in this fulfilling experience. You were constantly on my mind in the process, as I sought to make you proud. Amber, thank you for all the advice whenever I asked for it and listening whenever I needed it. Cindy, thank you for exposing me to books.

Last but not least, Quinn: my publisher told me to write this book so that a curious kid could understand it. You didn't even know it, but you were my muse in this writing journey. Thank you for being my inspiration, my reason for behaving like a role model, and straight up being my friend.

Every single one of you made this book better. Every single one of you made me better. Your contributions will help people solve their burning problems.

I love all of you.

Thank you.

ABOUT THE AUTHOR

Ted Harrington is the Executive Partner at Independent Security Evaluators (ISE), the company of ethical hackers famous for hacking cars, medical devices, and password managers. He's helped hundreds of companies fix tens of thousands of security vulnerabilities, including Google, Amazon, Microsoft, Netflix, and more. Ted has been featured in more than one hundred media outlets, including *The Wall Street Journal*, *Financial Times*, and *Forbes*. His team founded and organizes IoT Village, an event whose hacking contest has produced three DEF CON Black Badges.

To get help with security consulting and security assessments, or to book Ted to keynote your next event, visit *https:// www.tedharrington.com*.

GLOSSARY

Abuse Functionality: a technique that uses an application's own features to exploit vulnerabilities.

Accidental Insider: a type of adversary that is otherwise trustworthy and doesn't mean to harm your company. They just do something dumb. Accidental insiders are actually victims, too, but they are nevertheless the source of your breach.

Admin: the highest level of user privileges in a system.

Adversary: attacker.

Agile: an iterative software development process.

App: see Application.

Application: a program or piece of software that fulfills a particular purpose for a user. Also referred to as "app" or "system."

Application Programming Interface (**API**): a computing interface that specifies how software components should interact.

Application Security: The process of improving the security of an application by finding, fixing, and preventing security vulnerabilities. Application security covers all domains of an application, including software, code, executables, firmware, cloud deployments, third-party integrations, and application interfaces.

Assets: the tangible or intangible things your application protects.

Attack Surfaces: the points where data is transferred or accessed.

Authentication: the process by which a user proves who they are.

Authentication Bypass: a type of vulnerability that allows an attacker to access assets or resources without verifying identity.

Authorization: the process by which a system verifies a user's permissions.

Back End: the servers, databases, and other portions of an application that enable the user-facing front end.

Black-Box: a security-testing methodology that limits information in order to attempt to replicate real-world conditions.

Blockchain: a distributed ledger of transactions.

Bolt Security On: a bad security philosophy that postpones considering security until after the product is built and deployed.

Botnet: a network of compromised devices that are infected with malicious software and controlled as a group without the owners' knowledge.

Broken Access Control: a failure to enforce user's permissions.

Broken Authentication: a failure to verify user identity.

Broken Authorization: a failure to verify user's permissions.

Brute-Force Attack: a systematic process of attempting every possible decryption pair.

Buffer Overflow: a security vulnerability whereby attackers can corrupt memory in order to manipulate system functionality.

Bug Bounty Program: formalized crowdsourcing initiatives that reward security researchers for finding flaws in a company's technology.

Build Security In: a security philosophy that considers security at each stage of the development process.

Capability Gap: the distinction between security-testing efforts that are defined by low skill, low effort, and heavy reliance on automated tools versus security-testing efforts that are defined by high skill, high effort, and primarily manual investigation.

Casual Hacker: an adversary type that are defined as explorers, problem solvers, even anarchists. They see hacking as a challenge. They might not even be malicious; they just want to prove they can do it. Also known as individual hackers or small-group hackers.

Chain Exploits: to combine two or more vulnerabilities in order to multiply impact.

Cloud: refers to software that runs remotely on computers owned and controlled by a service provider.

Complete System Compromise: an attacker has entirely dominated your system and can do anything they want to it.

Corporate Espionage: an adversary type that attacks other companies in order to gain a competitive advantage, steal intellectual property, or save on research and development.

Critical Severity: the rating for a vulnerability that is readily exploitable, or substantially exposed and would deliver excessive damage.

Cross-Site Request Forgery (CSRF): a vulnerability where a third-party web page can trick a user's browser into sending unauthorized commands to web application.

Cross-Site Scripting (XSS): a vulnerability that enables attackers to inject malicious scripts into web pages viewed by other users.

Cryptocurrency Trading Platform: a system that stores a user's digital currency.

Cryptographic Algorithm: the mathematical process for encrypting and decrypting data.

Custom Exploit: an attack that is unique to the way your technology is designed and implemented.

Defense in Depth: a security approach that layers defenses in order to both minimize likelihood of breach and minimize damage resulting from a breach.

Design Flaw: when the system works exactly as intended and the attacker uses functionality to exploit the system.

Disgruntled Insider: a type of adversary that is motivated by revenge. They start as loyal people, but then something changes. As a result, they become angry and set out to hurt your company. Unlike accidental or opportunistic insiders, disgruntled insiders are malicious.

Domain Name System (DNS): a distributed database system that resolves IP addresses.

Efficiency Cliff: a steep decline in efficiency after too much time between activities.

Efficiency Gain: the more you do something, the faster you get at it.

Encryption Key: a small secret piece of information that the cryptographic algorithm uses to protect the larger stream of data.

Ethical Hacking: the act of probing technology for weaknesses by using the same tools and techniques that malicious actors use but with the intent of helping the subject rather than hurting it.

Exposure: a factor in rating the severity of a security vulnerability that considers how accessible a vulnerable system is and how easily an attack can be performed.

External Attacker: a category of adversaries that don't have any special privileges or access. There are five types: casual hackers, hacktivists, corporate espionage, organized crime, and nation-states.

False Positives: a vulnerability finding, typically from an automated scanner, which suggests there's a vulnerability where there's not one.

Front End: the portion of an application that users interact with.

General Data Protection Regulation 2016/679 (GDPR): a regulation on data protection and privacy in the European Union (EU) and the European Economic Area (EEA). It also regulates the transfer of personal data outside the EU and EEA.

Goldilocks Principle: you can invest too much or too little in trying to find security vulnerabilities; you need to find the best balance.

Hacker: someone who solves problems and makes things behave differently than intended. Ethical hackers do good, whereas attackers do bad.

Hacking: making something behave differently than it was intended to.

Hacktivist: an adversary type that attacks in order to draw attention to their cause. Hacktivists usually have an ideology and include terrorists who pursue ruthless causes.

Heartbleed: a security vulnerability in the open-source code library that implemented critical security protocols.

High Severity: the rating for a vulnerability that heavily exposes the system but demands additional attack requirements.

Impact: a factor in rating the severity of a security vulnerability that considers how valuable an asset is and how much damage results if the asset is compromised.

Implementation Flaw: when the system works differently than intended.

Info: the severity rating for a vulnerability that is unlikely to threaten the system. This designation provides important information to be aware of about issues that are not currently exploitable, but where future changes to the system may alter exposure or impact.

Input Sanitization: a defense technique that prevents an attacker from entering malicious data.

Insider Threat: a category of adversaries who have elevated trust and elevated access. There are four types of insider threats: accidental insider, opportunistic insider, disgruntled insider, and malicious insider.

Intangible Assets: conditions that can be undermined, such as system availability, authorized access to the system, integrity of your business model, reputation, or trust.

Internet Backbone: the array of high-speed networks that enable computer-to-computer traffic over the internet.

Internet of Things (IoT): the system of computing devices that's connected to the internet.

Internet Protocol (IP) Address: a unique number that identifies devices on a network.

Iterative Software Development: an approach to software development that breaks a large application project down into smaller chunks by cycling through requirements, design, implementation, testing, and deployment on each feature to be developed.

Kanban: an iterative software development process.

Kerckhoff's Principle: a system should be secure even if everything about the system (except the key) is public knowledge.

Kiosk Mode: a setting intended to prevent user interaction outside of the software.

Known Knowns: flaws that you know about and that impact you. These are the vulnerabilities you've discovered through security assessments.

Known Unknowns: flaws you know exist but may or may not impact you. These are the common vulnerabilities such as XSS, CSRF, or broken authentication, but you're not sure yet if they exist in your system.

Linear-Sequential: a software development methodology where the entire development project is approached as a whole with each phase being completed before the next phase begins.

Load Balancing: a process to distribute requests in web applications.

Low Severity: the rating for a vulnerability that delivers partial exposure but is not an immediate threat to the most valuable assets.

Malicious Insider: an adversary type that is an agent of an external group, often with access to that group's resources. They are motivated to harm the company. In some cases, the malicious insiders are already an agent when seeking a job or contract with you. In other cases, they're recruited later.

Medium Severity: the rating for a vulnerability that is not a significant risk to the system alone but could lead to exploitation if combined with other issues.

Mirai Botnet: a botnet is a network of compromised devices that are infected with malicious software and controlled as a group without the owners' knowledge. The Mirai botnet was used in an attack that made the internet unusable for huge portions of the East Coast of the United States.

Mitigations: remediations that minimize exploitability or reduce severity of the vulnerability.

Mitigation Testing: synonymous with remediation testing, which is the process by which you verify that the remediations you implemented are done right, solve the problem, and do not introduce new vulnerabilities.

Multifactor Authentication (MFA): a mechanism to prove identity that requires the user to successfully present two or more pieces of evidence before being granted access.

Nation-State: an adversary type that are countries who seek geopolitical advantage.

Native Applications: those built specifically for mobile or desktop use.

On-Premises: refers to software that runs on your physical site on computers you own and control.

Opportunistic Insider: an adversary type that is motivated to obtain some personal gain if—and only if—they think they can get away with it. They don't set out to harm your company, but if a good opportunity arises, they'll try.

Organized Crime: an adversary type who wants to make money.

Patch: a set of changes to a computer system that fixes a flaw in it.

Penetration Testing: a time-constrained effort to measure a single outcome. It's only suitable for mature, hardened systems.

Probability: how likely an attack will succeed. Probability is a key factor in calculating risk.

Rapid Application Development: an iterative software development process.

Rate Limiting: a technique that locks an account if too many failed log-in attempts are made.

Reassessment: a follow-up round of security testing that entails all of the same elements as an initial assessment, including run scans, look for known vulnerabilities, abuse functionality, daisy chain vulnerabilities, and seek the unknowns.

Red Teaming: a test of your security team's response capabilities.

Remediations: solutions to your vulnerabilities. They come either as resolutions (which completely fix the flaw) or as mitigations (which minimize exploitability or reduce severity).

Remediation Plan: the plan and timing for when your developers will fix discovered vulnerabilities.

Remediation Testing: the process by which you verify that the remediations you implemented are done right, solve the problem, and do not introduce new vulnerabilities.

Remote Code Execution (RCE) Vulnerability: a security flaw that enables an attacker to execute commands or code, thereby controlling how the system behaves.

Request Smuggling: an attack technique that abuses discrepancies in how different pieces of software process inputs.

Resolutions: remediations that completely fix the vulnerability.

Reverse Engineering: a process used by both ethical hackers and real-world attackers to deconstruct a component in order to learn how it works, in order to figure out how to defeat it.

Risk: a computation of probability that an attack will succeed multiplied by the resulting impact if it does.

Scrum: an iterative software development process.

Security Assessment: an umbrella term for all varieties of security testing intended to improve the security of a piece of technology.

Security Consultant: a subject matter expert who can help you solve your application security problems, including testing, design, coding, security principles, and how to use security to win sales. Used interchangeably with terms including security evaluator, security assessor, security expert, or security partner.

Security Consulting: a professional service that helps solve complex security engineering problems.

Security Excellence: a mindset that is defined by the relentless pursuit of better.

Security Questionnaire: an attempt by your customer to document security posture, policies, and controls. The purpose is to understand the risk they'd be taking on by engaging with a supplier.

Security through Obscurity: an invalid security philosophy that relies on secrecy as the primary defense mechanism.

Security Vulnerability: a weakness an attacker can exploit in order to perform unauthorized actions within a computer system.

Sequential Identifiers: a strategic weakness that makes it easy to predict sensitive account information, because account numbers are assigned in order.

Severity: a rating of how significant a given security vulnerability is. Severity ratings balance many factors and help you determine how to prioritize remediations.

Social Engineering: an attack technique using psychological manipulation to trick people into taking actions they otherwise shouldn't.

System: see Application.

Tangible Assets: material things that can be stolen, such as personally identifiable information (PII), customer data, business intelligence, or money.

Threat: attacker.

Threat Model: an analysis of the assets you want to protect, the adversaries you want to defend against, and the attack surfaces they'll try to exploit.

Unknown Unknowns: flaws so unexpected you don't even consider them. This comes in numerous forms, including novel versions of common vulnerabilities, previously unknown attack methods, and zero-days in the supply chain.

User Story: refers to a software feature described from an end user's perspective.

Vulnerability Assessment: A vulnerability assessment is a comprehensive, rigorous, manual effort to discover security vulnerabilities, assign severity ratings to them, and determine how to fix them. The objective is to find as many as possible and remediate them. As a result, you understand and reduce risk. The ideas in this book are built around this model.

Vulnerability Scanning: a low-cost, low-effort exercise to quickly find basic issues by using an automated tool. It includes false positives and inappropriate severity ratings.

Waterfall: a linear-sequential software development methodology.

Web Application: the type of application that is built to use via a web browser.

White-Box: a security-testing methodology that maximizes information sharing in order to maximize the output value of the assessment.

XSS: see Cross-Site Scripting.

Zero-Day: the type of catastrophic vulnerability that you have literally zero days to fix because it's exploitable in the wild right now.

BIBLIOGRAPHY

B. R., Shubhamangala, and Snehanshu Saha. "Application Security Risk: Assessment and Modeling." *ISACA Journal* 2 (March 2016). https://www.isaca.org/Journal/archives/2016/volume-2/Pages/application-security-risk.aspx.

Communication Theory. "The Johari Window Model." September 30, 2020. https://www.communicationtheory.org/the-johari-window-model/.

Franceschi-Bicchiera, Lorenzo. "For 20 Years, This Man Has Survived Entirely by Hacking Online Games." *Motherboard*, July 29, 2020. https://www.vice.com/en_us/article/59p7qd/this-man-has-survived-by-hacking-mmo-online-games.

Franceschi-Bicchiera, Lorenzo. "Hackers Are Selling a Critical Zoom Zero-Day Exploit for $500,000." *Motherboard*, April 15, 2020. https://www.vice.com/en_us/article/qjdqgv/hackers-selling-critical-zoom-zero-day-exploit-for-500000.

Greenberg, Andy. "A 'Blockchain Bandit' Is Guessing Private Keys and Scoring Millions." *Wired*, April 23, 2019. https://www.wired.com/story/blockchain-bandit-ethereum-weak-private-keys/.

Independent Security Evaluators. "Exploiting the iPhone." July 12, 2017. https://www.ise.io/casestudies/exploiting-the-iphone/.

Independent Security Evaluators. "Securing Hospitals." February 23, 2016. https://www.ise.io/hospitalhack/.

Independent Security Evaluators. "The Blockchain Bandit: Finding over 700 Active Private Keys on Ethereum's Blockchain." YouTube, April 23, 2019. https://www.ise.io/casestudies/ethercombing/.

Jones, Capers. *Applied Software Management: Assuring Productivity and Quality*. New York: McGraw-Hill, 1996.

Miessler, Daniel. "The Difference between a Vulnerability Assessment and a Penetration Test." *DavidMiessler.com*, December 17, 2019. https://danielmiessler.com/study/vulnerability-assessment-penetration-test/.

Turkel, Bruce. *All About Them: Grow Your Business by Focusing on Others*. Boston: Da Capo Lifelong Books, 2016.

Wilson, Michael. "Adventures of the 'Wolverine' Leaker." *The New York Times*, January 12, 2010. https://www.nytimes.com/2010/01/13/nyregion/13wolverine.html.